Socialites

and

Scofflaws

| Avon Lake's Past |

Sherry Newman Spenzer

For Heritage Avon Lake

Acknowledgments

With deepest gratitude to the following, whose contributions to this book all made pieces of Avon Lake's history come alive:

Edith Newman, for her patiently rendered and artfully drawn sketches

Thomas J. Patton, Bernadette Hisey, and Carl "Timer" Tomanek for sharing and allowing reprints from their photo collections

Heritage Avon Lake and the Avon Lake Public Library for photos provided from their collections

Karl Brunjes and Connor Beach for the contributions of their original photography

Laura Ploenzke for her skillful proof-reading assistance

Tony Tomanek, Gerry Vogel and Melissa Clifford for their encouragement and support in the creation of this book

Daniel Vasu, guardian of my literary efforts, who saves me from my technological failings, and has ushered this book into existence

Contents

Preface

Socialites – they were a city's prominent citizens who busied themselves with social, charitable and artistic affairs, urging culture and refinement of taste upon their communities. Scofflaws were their antagonists – remorseless transgressors who stirred civic reproach while capturing community attention with unconventional and antisocial behavior. Some simply skirted the edges of civility, while others openly defied governing norms and wrote their own rules.

Avon Lake's shore drew its full measure of extremes. Farmers grappled with intruding vacationers and the Lake Shore Electric Railway. Socialites used the shore as their venue for clubs and organizations focused on service, enlightenment, and entertainment that commanded the notice of the society pages of newspapers. The Lake Shore Electric Railway fostered Beach Park, a "sub-city" that provided housing for employees, an amusement park, a dance hall, and outdoor recreational facilities. All were intended to stimulate commercial development of the line. Bold rum-runners found efficient transport of illegally imported alcohol by way of Lake Erie's Avon Point and other locations along the shore during Prohibition, but sometimes at the high cost of violent loss of lives. Even a mobster of local notoriety found some degree of escape from constant scrutiny when he quietly relocated to Avon Lake's shore.

It is this contrast of extremes that forms the very substance of Avon Lake's provocative past. Lives lived both publicly and privately all contributed to the shaping of their community's existence. Some left a legacy of industry and progress. Others left stories of daring and danger. All left their histories to the successive generations of the City of Avon Lake.[1]

Lake Shore Electric Railway Car.
Photo courtesy of Thomas J. Patton

[1] Reference to "Avon Lake" shall be used throughout this book simply for consistency and ease of reading. Blind endnotes are provided at the conclusion of the book for those interested in examining original sources.

Chapter 1

Growing Pains

The earliest recorded settlement of the wilds of northern Avon - later to secede and become Avon Lake - was the solitary lean-to of pioneer Noah Davis in 1812. He stayed less than a year, then abandoned his primitive abode. Though Davis chose not to remain, others discovered the farming opportunities afforded by Avon Lake's fertile fields. Those who succeeded him settled and tilled the land running south from Erie's shore, fruit farms were cultivated, and vineyards thrived in soil particularly well-suited to grape growing.

Expansion boomed with a turn-of-the-century influx of vacationers seeking relief offered by the lake shore on sultry summer days. With the introduction of the Lake Shore Electric Railway in 1893, sales of farmland drew far greater profits than did sales of crops. Summer cottages sprang up in areas offering pedestrian access to Lake Erie's shore. Cottage clusters at such locations as "Stop 45"[2] of the Lake Shore Electric formed, offering charming summer residences with porches that captured lake breezes and allowed seasonal occupants access to beaches that were just a short walk away.

---

[2] Lake Shore Electric Railway traversed Electric Boulevard, with a series of numbered stops throughout the city. Stop 45 was located at South Point Drive in Avon Lake. The location has retained its moniker, and continues as a means of identifying that area of the city among longtime residents.

With its economic development, the northernmost portion of Avon Township grew restless in its desire to separate from the southern township's farming community. Politically, the township was split, with the northern portion of the community being predominantly Republican, and the southern portion being mostly Democrat. Efforts to secede began in the early 1900s.

As the lake shore's residents agitated for independence, southern Avon-ites in 1905 threatened court proceedings to enjoin any bifurcation of the township. The drive for secession was undeterred, and in July 1911, an election was held by order of the Trustees of the Township of Avon which resulted in the separation of northern and southern Avon Township. Two new entities emerged, and were laterally divided by the tracks of the Nickel Plate Railroad. At an election on November 7, 1911, village officers for the newly formed Avon Lake were chosen, and they assumed their offices on January 1, 1912.

The new entity's continuing evolution was a turbulent one. As construction of a brick highway across the northern end of the county posed a prospective financial burden upon Avon Lake, the village sought to surrender its charter and revert to township status to avoid the assessment. At a special election in August 1914, the charter was surrendered.

In 1917, Avon and Avon Lake locked horns in a battle for collection of taxes from the portion of Nickel Plate Railroad's right of way that divided the two townships. On the same day in April 1917, each entity voted for independent incorporation, with Avon Lake once again assuming village status. Both villages claimed entitlement to the railroad easement and the tax revenue that would result, and the matter was brought before the county's court.

In June of 1917, Avon Lake prevailed, and its financial future loomed even brighter. Avon Lake grew into an entertainment mecca as the 1920's roared. An influx of entertainment-seeking vacationers quickly fueled development of the "Beach Park" establishment funded by Lake Shore Electric profits, drawing patrons from cities both east and west.

The lake's temperate summer climate drew more than just picnickers and cottagers. A wealthier class of successful Clevelanders discovered the area's appeal, bought prime lakeshore property, and established "summer country homes", which were given names and received frequent mention in the society pages of Cleveland newspapers. Avon Lake successfully endured the Depression years, but many summer cottages were upgraded to serve as "year round" housing, the finer country homes disappeared, and developments predominated. Lake Erie's health has vacillated, but its wildlife thrives and Avon Lake's sunsets continue to draw admirers to the shore.

Chapter 2

The Encroaching Elite

As metropolitan businesses boomed, the quality of life for those who sought success in urban settings exacted its price. At an 1866 meeting of a group formed as the Lake Shore Grape Growers Association, one member of the organization described the lives of those in the juice and wine making business as "life-prisoners, confined in the four walls of stores and offices". He bemoaned the "monotonous drudgery of business by day and night", with "no more variation than that of a horse on a treadmill". The speaker described one of the commonalities amongst city businessmen as a loss of vision for the beauties of nature, and emphasized the need for frequent visits away from usual pursuits for the sake of one's health and the development of dormant faculties.

The need for relief from deprivation of the things of nature stirred a well-to-do contingent of city folk to seek "farms" and temporary residences in rural locations, and Avon Lake offered some choice real estate locations in bucolic settings. One of the early investors to be drawn to the lake's shore was C.W. Johnston, a doctor-turned-lawyer with a successful law practice in bustling Elyria, Ohio. The barrister found Avon Point and its prime vineyard soil to be the antidote to the demands of city life. He purchased acreage there in mid-1800 where he established a summer home, cultivated grapes, and hosted gatherings of viticulturists.

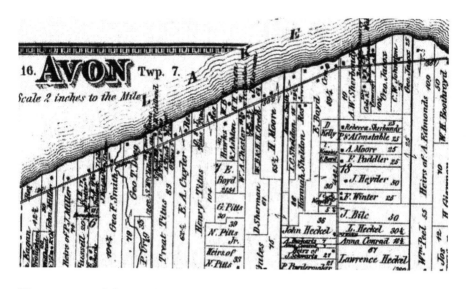

The property of C.W. Johnston appears on this 1874 map of Avon Lake at Avon Point, the northernmost point of the shoreline

Other successful industrialists and professionals from Elyria and Cleveland were also drawn to the shore, but not all felt a need to undertake agricultural pursuits. They purchased acreage for "country estates" along Erie's shore, and an elite society made itself welcome. Socialites occupying these seasonal homes used them as summer escapes and entertainment venues for a variety of clubs, socials, and prominent guests. To further distinguish these homes from the more diminutive summer cottages occupied by middle-class vacationers, the owners gave names to their residences, a tradition steeped in British history. While the British sought to maintain ancestral identity in naming their manors, halls, and abbeys, some of the names borne by Avon Lake's more lavish summer homes were inspired by location, some incorporated the owners' names, and some appeared to reflect simply a bit of whimsy.

Among the earlier residents to appropriate prime lake shore property for summer escape was the Sayle family of Cleveland. In 1888, Mrs. Walter D. Sayle and her sister-in-law made society columns when the former chose a site at Avon Point for her summer residence. She christened the spot "To Kalon Beach". The name was Greek, meaning "most beautiful" or "the highest beauty". To Kalon was also the name given to a Napa Valley vineyard planted in 1868, known for its production of outstanding red grapes.

Cleveland newspaper society pages were vigilant in tracking the seasonal occupancy of Mrs. Sayle, her various female family members, and their children as they migrated to To Kalon each summer through 1890. Less frequently sighted at To Kalon was Mr. Sayle – banker turned successful industrialist – as newspaper society pages only occasionally mentioned his presence at the family's summer escape.

Sayle served as director of Midland Bank, and was a founder of East End Savings Bank Co., which later merged with the Cleveland Trust Company. He then became president and manager of the Cleveland Punch and Shear Works, and procured three additional companies that were integral to Punch and Shear's support and operations. While Sayle devoted his hours to industry, To Kalon remained, it appears, the primary province of his wife and her kin.

Sketch of Walter D. Sayle by Edith Newman

Though the Sayles used their summer home as simply a hot weather family retreat, other seasonal residents expanded use of their lake shore "country estates" as venues for club gatherings, entertainment of friends, and in one instance, even employees. Mr. and Mrs. John Goetz were among those who used their summer lake home to both personal and business advantage.

In 1898, the family of John Goetz made society news when they opened and occupied their Avon Lake summer residence at the Lake Shore Electric's Stop 44[3] at Avon Lake's east end. They christened their place "Felseneck", a name also associated with wine – a Reisling produced in southwest Germany. John Goetz was a successful retailer on Pearl Street in Cleveland, hailed by the *Cleveland Leader* newspaper as one of a few men in Cleveland who had grown substantially with the city in the millinery business, with a store that "has earned a substantial reputation among Cleveland ladies". His establishment boasted the very latest in hats, bonnets, and millinery, and enjoyed a "reputation for high class talent in the workroom".

Sketch of John Goetz by Edith Newman

---

[3] Stop 44 is located near Tomahawk Drive in Avon Lake.

Hats and bonnets no doubt decorated the Goetz lake shore home and grounds when employees of the latter's store were invited there for a day of summer entertainment in July of 1898. First to descend upon Felseneck were the ladies of the millinery department, followed next by the women of the "ladies' furnishing department" for successive days of summer enjoyment.

John and his wife continued use of their summer home for several decades, and place of death was listed simply as "Avon Lake" on John Goetz's death certificate at the time of his demise on October 10, 1919. The home remained in the Goetz family for more than a decade, as son Robert and his wife continued hosting at the residence well into the 1930's.

Another dwelling to grace Avon Lake's shore boasted deep historic roots. Bearing the lengthy name "Lilac Ledges, Reidlands", the home was located north of Avon Lake's existing Parsons Drive. Accessible via Stop 49 of the LSE Railway, Lilac Ledges was owned by David E. and Mary Reid Parsons. Mr. Parsons enjoyed a successful career as general manager of the Strong-Carlisle-Hammond Company in Cleveland. It was Mrs. Parsons, however, who received frequent mention in society columns hailing both her ancestry and her home's history.

Mrs. Parsons regularly hosted members of the John S. Reid Chapter of the United States Daughters of 1812 at Lilac Ledges, John S. Reid being her grandfather. She identified her Avon Lake residence as being more than 100 years old, claiming its location to be the site of her grandfather John Reid's former home. Reid had distinguished himself as one of Ohio's first Commissioners, as well as first postmaster and Justice of the Peace in Black River (Lorain).

The second floor of the Parsons' historic home was tragically ravaged by fire in 1927, with a news account of the incident describing total destruction of "tapestries, heirlooms, antiques and laces" valued at over $12,000. Bay Village and Dover fire departments were of limited help, and Avon Lake's department had exhausted its entire supply of chemical fire stop, along with three wells and two cisterns in attempting to control the blaze. Lake water could not be accessed, as the house was situated on a thirty-six foot cliff, depriving the department of opportunity to make use of the unreachable resource. The couple remained residents of Lilac Ledges, however - Mrs. Parsons until her death in November 1930, and Mr. Parsons until his death in July 1934.

Joining the industrialist and retailer on Avon Lake's prime lakeshore properties were Colonel and Mrs. Allan T. Brinsmade, who named their summer home Cliffhurst-on-the-Lake. With its name reminiscent of a manor in a Charlotte Bronte novel, Cliffhurst served first as a summer home, then as a year-round residence. Located at the eastern end of the Coveland Drive horseshoe where it adjoins Lake Road in Avon Lake, it housed two generations of Brinsmades. At the time of Colonel Brinsmade's death in 1913, he was hailed as being Ohio's second oldest practicing lawyer and a Civil War veteran. He and his wife, Anna, had occupied Cliffhurst at least as early as 1909.

Sketch of Alan T. Brinsmade by Edith Newman

The Colonel had been active politically, serving first as City Attorney for Cleveland, then as State Senator from 1872 to 1874, and later as U.S. District

Attorney under President Harrison. Anna Brinsmade died at Cliffhurst in August of 1910. Her husband died three years later in November of 1913. Prior to his death, Colonel Brinsmade had shared a law practice with his son, Thomas C. Brinsmade, a colorful character who became Cliffhurst's next occupant.

Thomas had drawn unflattering press in 1901 with news of an assault on his first wife, Lillian, while he was in an inebriated state. The couple was living in the home of Lillian's father. They quarreled viciously following an evening out, and Lillian's cries drew her father's attention. Thomas was reduced to a very poor physical condition once his father-in-law intervened. A battered Brinsmade was charged with assault, and was taken to jail where he spent the evening. The next morning, the assistant prosecuting attorney contacted the judge on Brinsmade's behalf, and the latter was released without even so much as personal bond being posted. Police investigation did not produce nearly as much detail as did sensational news articles that recounted the incident. When questioned, Lillian's father responded, "Trouble at my house last night? What do you mean? What are you talking about"?

The following week, charges against Brinsmade were dropped. The same assistant prosecuting attorney who secured the defendant's release announced that the case had been dismissed. His explanation to the press was that there was not enough testimony to secure a conviction.

Brinsmade's woes had begun several months earlier when he was stripped of the position of Cleveland police prosecutor in May of 1901. Serving under Cleveland Mayor Herman Baehr, Brinsmade was not reappointed when there was a change in elected officials that spring.

Claiming relief at his release from the position, which had in the past been held by his father, Brinsmade joined the latter in a father and son law practice. He ran for state representative in 1901, but was among those candidates who were "blacklisted" by the Anti-Saloon League and the Federation of Church Clubs for reason of his "attitude" on the "liquor question". These pre-prohibition activists proved themselves to be formidable foes, and Brinsmade's bid for office failed.

Thomas Brinsmade also made brief news for his "stage inclinations" in his performance with a "troupe of minstrels" in 1907, and in 1909, he posted an ad seeking investors willing to invest capital in "a great proposition . . . in the amusement line". In September of 1910, Lillian was granted a divorce from Thomas on grounds of neglect, Mrs. Brinsmade testifying to her husband's frequent absences from home requiring her to return to the home of her father with their daughter.

Sketch of Thomas Brinsmade
by Edith Newman

In April 1912, Thomas re-married, and the couple made Cliffhurst their primary residence. Brinsmade focused his full talents on criminal defense work, where he seemingly found outlets for both his theatrical propensities and his rebellious nature. His obituary lauded him as defender of "more persons in city and county criminal courts than any other lawyer in the history of the [Cleveland] bar". His death certificate lists his residence address as 32212 Lake Road in Avon Lake, giving a more precise location to the shore's Cliffhurst-on-the-Lake.

Another summer estate home, built at Stop 46 of Lake Road, was fittingly named "Bellmar" by its owners, George C. and Grace Cothe Bell. Mr. Bell was the owner of a shop in Cleveland that produced carriages for many of that city's prominent families. As the automobile gained popularity, the business evolved into a dealership for Ford cars. In Bell's later years, he involved himself in real estate development until the time of his death.

Bellmar's initial location was identified simply as "Stop 46"[4], but its address appears in a later Avon Lake directory as 32114 Lake Road. The lake shore home served as an entertainment site for the couple's dinners and dances, but was more frequently used by Mrs. Bell in hosting a variety of clubs in which she was involved.

*Sketch of Grace C. Bell
by Edith Newman*

---

[4] Stop 46 is at Lear Road in Avon Lake.

Chapter 3

Avon Point – The Final Destination

Retreat-seeking socialites migrated faithfully each summer to their much-loved country homes at the lake's shore, but Erie's esteem for the socialites was not returned in equal measure. The lake could, at times, be an unforgiving tyrant. Disaster was visited upon rich and poor alike, and Erie's Avon Point did not play favorites. Avon Point was the site of lost loads of ore, coal, lumber, limestone and other cargo. Even the most seasoned of lake boat captains was no match for fickle Erie's unannounced gales of destruction. Loss of property could spell financial devastation for seafarers, but even more tragic was the loss of lives that Erie wrought, and fortune was poor protection from tempestuous Erie.

One of the early recorded Avon Point disasters was that of the June 21, 1868 collision of the steamship Morning Star and the barque Cortland. The Morning Star had departed Cleveland between 9:00 and 10:30 p.m. on a Saturday evening, and was transporting approximately 40 passengers and a crew of 30 from Cleveland to Detroit. The Cortland was making the reverse voyage with a load of ore. A rainy mist and choppy waters sent many of the steamship's passengers early to their cabins the evening of June 20. Shortly before 1:00 a.m. the next day, the Morning Star's captain observed the white lights of other vessels traveling the same direction. Visibility was poor, and to ensure ample clearance, the Morning Star made a slight adjustment to its course – a move that spelled immediate disaster.

The Cortland's mate, noticing that the barque's outside green lantern had gone dim, took it inside to trim the wick. Just as he returned to replace the light, the temporarily unlit Cortland and the Morning Star collided, tearing a hole in the Morning Star's bow, and another in the side of the Cortland. The mate was killed instantly by the impact.

The Morning Star's descent into 65 feet of water was rapid. By some survivors' accounts, the ship sunk in 5 minutes' time. Other reports held that its descent took 15 minutes. All told the same story of cries and screams filling the waters off Avon Point, as debris from the ship and pieces of luggage and furniture were tossed about by the waves. Some escaped in lifeboats, some clung to pieces of the ship's debris and were rescued by vessels that came to render aid, and some were not found until their bodies were washed ashore. The effort to rescue any remaining survivors was abandoned on Sunday evening as the weather had grown too fierce. An exact count of lives lost was never determined. While the ship's log listed the names of paying passengers, emigrants and children were not all documented, with total losses remaining forever unknown.

For those of wealth and connection, search reports were carried in numerous newspapers. The Patchin sisters were among those most frequently mentioned. Caroline and Mary Patchin, 23 and 20 years old respectively, had traveled from Troy, New York to Cleveland for the wedding of their cousin, Isabelle Tiffany. Caroline was one of Isabelle's 6 bridesmaids in a ceremony held at Trinity Church on June 17, 1868.

Following the wedding, the Patchin sisters boarded the Morning Star to Detroit to visit some friends before returning home. Upon learning of the Morning Star's destruction, the girls' brother, A.D. Patchin, who had been with them at the wedding, went in immediate search of his sisters or their remains. He, a cousin, and an assemblage of compassionate friends combed the beach from Black River (Lorain) to Avon Point looking for the bodies. Their efforts were unrewarded, but a trunk identified as belonging to one of the sisters was later recovered at Black River on June 23. Other Morning Star wreckage that began washing ashore littered the beaches from Black River to 5 miles east of Cleveland.

Pleas for aid in recovery of those believed deceased were issued in multiple locales. In Ashtabula, the following request was printed in the local newspaper:

> "The friends of those who were lost in consequence of this accident will feel very grateful for any information leading to the recovery of bodies, and trust the citizens from Black River to Fairport will observe the service of the lake each day, more closely than usual, believing all the bodies will be recovered. Any information sent or telegraphed to this office will be promptly published."

On September 18, 1868, Caroline's remains were found washed ashore on a beach at Long Point, Ontario. Not until October 22 was Mary's corpse recovered, when it was found ashore at Painesville. One news report described the loss of the siblings poignantly:

"Lake Erie's waves chant a requiem over many a loved and beautiful thing – but none more loved and beautiful than the two young souls so cruelly snatched from our midst."

Another loss was that of Albert Iddings, whose drowning was described as "one of the saddest of the many sad cases connected with the late horror." Described as handsome, amiable, and full of happy hope, he was en route to Detroit to visit his fiancée. His body was pulled from the water by a tug near the site of the Avon Point wreck. His brother, George, was aboard the tug at the time of recovery. Albert's new silk top hat had been found by divers just weeks prior.

No inquest was conducted concerning the Morning Star-Cortland incident, as the matter was regarded as being entirely accidental. An outspoken journalist felt quite differently about the Avon Point disaster, and boldly expressed the following opinion:

". . . in accidents by rail or boat there is never any blame attached to anybody – but it was a 'dispensation of Divine Providence'. That is the way it will be fixed finally, and in the meantime corporations will go on murdering the traveling community with none to molest or make afraid. No one responsible for the loss of twenty valuable, lives, the most of them women. It reads well."

Tragic loss of human life again struck in 1900, devastating the Corrigan family, when the famed sailing yacht *Idler* also met its demise at Avon Point, with heavy losses to brothers John and James Corrigan of Cleveland. The siblings shared in ownership of Corrigan-McKinney Steel, the successful culmination of a series of business undertakings. Both men were skilled sailors with extensive experience.

In 1899, John became owner of the *Idler*. The ninety-seven foot sailing vessel boasted handsome cabins for guests, and quarters for the captain and a crew of 6 men. John Corrigan had chosen Captain Charles Holmes to pilot the craft for the 1900 sailing season.

A joint family excursion was undertaken in the last week of June 1900. On board were James Corrigan, wife Ida, daughters Jane, Ida, Nettie (Mrs. Charles) Rieley, and Nettie's baby, Mary. John Corrigan's guests included wife Mary, daughter Etta, and another daughter and son-in-law, Mr. and Mrs. Edward Gilbert.

Though the excursionists were not due to return to Cleveland for several days, the number remaining on board was diminishing. James departed the ship early to see his doctor for an ear problem. John left to attend to a business matter. The Gilberts disembarked for a social engagement, and the remaining family members awaited return passage home.

Those of early departure escaped with their lives. On July 7, 1900, Lake Erie once again displayed her unpredictable temper with a vicious squall. Captain Holmes made the risky decision to leave all of the ship's sails up, confident that he could navigate the oncoming storm. Winds reached 60 to 65 miles per hour, and the yacht began to falter.

Despite the pleas of the Captain and other crew members, the Corrigan women refused to leave their cabins below ship and come to the deck so that rescue efforts could be attempted. In an effort to at least save baby Mary, one member of the crew pleaded with the child's mother to let him take the infant topside. According to later reports, the mother answered with "No! When I go, the baby goes!"

In a later scramble, a cork couch floated by and Etta nudged her mother onto it. Mrs. John Corrigan was the only family member to survive the disaster. The Captain and crew were all, however, spared the finality of a watery grave.

Almost immediately after learning of the disaster, the Corrigan brothers hastened to Avon Point to the tragic scene and enlisted tugboats and divers to begin the grisly task of retrieving bodies from the wreck. Again, Lake Erie refused cooperation, and initial efforts were thwarted by the weather. A diver sealed the door and hatchway of the vessel with nails and battings to preserve its contents and any bodies, and the Avon Point site was marked with lanterns for a later return.

Further recovery efforts resumed the following day, and with the aid of a seasoned diver, the body of Mrs. James Corrigan was retrieved from the wreckage. Next were the bodies of twenty-four-year old Nettie Corrigan Rieley, James Corrigan's daughter, and eighteen-year-old Etta Corrigan, John Corrigan's daughter. All were transported from Avon Point to Cleveland, where undertaker wagons, which had been summoned by carrier pigeons, came to take the bodies. Etta's funeral was held promptly after discovery of her remains, and she was buried at Woodland Cemetery.

The bodies of Mrs. James Corrigan and Mrs. Rieley, however, were kept in a vault for storage. Burial was deferred at James' insistence until the remaining family members were found and all could be buried together. Success eluded searchers at Avon Point as to the remaining bodies, and James Corrigan made arrangements to have the *Idler* towed to Cleveland to continue inspection of its interior. Only the body of baby Mary was found after the *Idler*'s arrival there.

James was both frantic and relentless in finding the remains of his loved ones. At his behest, newspapers in Cleveland carried notices under "Lost and Found", with the following offer:

REWARD

A liberal reward will be paid for the recovery of the bodies of the Misses Jane and Ida Corrigan, drowned off yacht Idler, near Cleveland, July 7. Wire any information to James Corrigan, Perry-Payne bldg., Cleveland, O.

James had also instigated a private investigation of the matter of the loss of the Idler and those on board by his personal lawyer. A dispute between Cuyahoga County Coroner and Lorain County Coroner ensued as to the issue of jurisdiction over an inquest. The latter contended that it was his province, as the ship had sunk at a Lorain County location.

The wreckage was towed 16 miles to Cleveland, a process that took 35 hours, and ultimately the wrangling was ended and the disagreement concluded when jurisdiction was relinquished to the Cuyahoga County Coroner. The relentless search continued without success until the body of fifteen-year-old Ida Corrigan was recovered August 29, 1900 after being spotted floating in the water, near where she had met death, by a steamer's passenger. Physical indications suggested that her remains had been trapped at the bottom of the lake, where the body had been pinned until its eventual release. It was towed in a small boat by tug from Avon Point to Cleveland. Twenty-two-year old Jane Corrigan's body was not found until nearly a month later on September 28 after it had washed ashore in Lake County.

After spending over $10,000 on the relentless search, and continuing the newspaper ads offering recompense for the recovery of any remains, all of James Corrigan's family members' bodies were finally recovered. James finally allowed the interment to proceed after his wife, daughters, and granddaughter had all been found. They were buried together on October 9, 1900, in Lakeview Cemetery in Cleveland. After widespread publicity of the Corrigan nightmare ceased, recollection of Avon Point's association with the tragedy dimmed, but history of the event's location remains unchanged.

Graves at Lakeview Cemetery of members of the Corrigan family who perished on the yacht Idler on July 7, 1900 at Avon Point. The upper row shows the graves of Mrs. Charles Rieley and her baby, Mary. Mrs. James Corrigan is the center grave, and daughters Jane and Ida appear in the photos directly below. Photos by Sherry Spenzer

Chapter 4

A Scrap of the Better Life

While country homes served foremost as escapes for wealthy city-dwellers who sought respite from urban heat, dust, and doldrums, some residents succumbed to conscience insofar as opening their homes for short periods to children who were deprived of even life's simplest pleasures. In 1889, an organization known as Fresh Air Camp was formed by "Father" Addison, a mildly eccentric but kindly gentleman concerned with the welfare of economically deprived children.

In 1895, an "outing department" was established. Persons feeling "benevolently disposed" were invited to open their homes, or at least contribute second-hand clothes or funds for the unfortunates. As early as 1898, some country homeowners of the greater Avon area shared a bit of their largesse by participating in the program, which provided two weeks of "vacation" for city children ranging from 6 to 12 years of age.

The children were described as being from the poorest city homes, where meals were not shared together by the family, houses were crowded and dark, and shabby clothing was worn. "Turned loose" to play in the dust and dirt of the city streets, children qualifying as Fresh Air candidates were described as having been left to "develop traits of character much different from those developed by country children".

It was hoped by Fresh Air organizers that the children's "right standard of living" might be improved by a two-week stay in the homes of generous volunteers. The youth would then be returned home after a two weeks' stay "tanned and happy".

The project involved the "tagging" of pre-qualified children by Fresh Air Camp officials with each child's name, address, and the identity of the persons who would be hosting them. A group of fifteen or twenty children would arrive at a designated depot, where the hosts were to find the child or children consigned to them. They were required to take their pre-assigned child, and were prohibited from engaging in any "picking" of their temporary charges.

Whether the two-week stints achieved their desired long-term effect remains unknown, but one Avon Lake socialite found it more expedient to devote herself to a project of longer commitment to children of limited opportunity. Created by the education division of the Federation of Women's Clubs, a later program was established to raise funds for students of academic promise who lacked the financial support to remain in school.

A qualifying student had to be of "good mentality, good character, ambitious and in every way worthy of a good education, but handicapped by home conditions". The mission was to help the child complete an education in the face of financial adversity and the pressure to quit school and secure employment.

The club women appointed themselves as "godmothers" to students accepted into the program. Each godmother was to maintain contact with her "protégé", visit the child in his or her home, and help the child to achieve academic success. One Avon Lake woman particularly devoted to the program was Marie C. Weigel, schoolteacher and a founder of the Avon Lake Garden Club.

Marie and her husband, Edward J. Weigel, owned a summer home in Avon Lake, but there was no name associated with her summer place. She hosted the annual picnic for the student protégés at her country estate on the lake shore, where students celebrated their success with their sponsors, to whom they had become "very much attached". Mrs. Weigel, a graduate of the school of education of Western Reserve University in Cleveland, was active in a multitude of clubs, and was an aviation enthusiast. Passionate about education, the socialite's efforts to keep children in school likely resulted in a more substantial return than the two-week country visits offered the Fresh Air campers in need of improved "traits of character".

Chapter 5

Coveting Thy Neighbor's Goods

Occupation of Avon Lake's shore by vacationing Clevelanders was sometimes known to stir envy, and even incite criminal conduct among laboring locals. Such was the case with Mary Gilmore and socialites George and Ellen Smith. George was owner of a movie theater in Cleveland, and a successful business man who fit easily into the lake shore league. Mary Gilmore - also known as Minnie - was a laundress, and an immigrant who had given birth to at least ten children. Born in Germany, she came to the United States in 1863. According to the 1910 U.S. Census, Mary was unable to write. At the age of 50, she still had several minor children in her home, and did her best to support them.

Mary's difficulties escalated in November of 1909 when she surrendered to the temptation unwittingly laid before her by Mrs. Smith. The socialite, apparently giving little thought to her actions, had tucked a small chamois bag containing $70 in cash and over $2,000 worth of diamond jewels into one of her silk stockings. The stockings were deposited into the laundry, which was then consigned to the washerwoman, Mary.

Upon discovering her employer's error, Mary confiscated the goods. When the loss was exposed, Mary became the target of a law enforcement investigation. She readily admitted to appropriating the cash, but told deputies she had tossed the gems into Lake Erie. The lost treasure was never found, and conflicting theories were developed as to the true disposition of Mrs. Smith's diamonds.

Some Avon Lakers believed that Mary, envious of Mrs. Smith's excess, simply wanted to possess some fine goods herself, but was then overcome by her conscience and hastily disposed of the purloined items. Others, including Judge Washburn, who was assigned to Mary's case, believed Mary had hidden the jewels, or passed them off to someone else, to be retrieved at a later time. Still others believed Mary's story for the unflattering reason that the woman was simply too ignorant to stick with her contention that the gems were in the lake unless it were true.

When Mary appeared in court for sentencing, the Judge imposed an eighteen-month prison sentence, which he then suspended so that the defendant might reflect upon her deed and perhaps recall the location of the jewels. Mary Gilmore returned to her menial labors and the support of her family with no further criminal incident on her part. After nearly a year had elapsed, Mary found herself face-to-face with a deputy sheriff in a neighbor's barn where she was at the task of husking corn. The unsuspecting woman, dressed in old, tattered clothing and rubber boots, was placed under arrest and delivered to Judge Washburn's courtroom.

The judge, wearied by the woman's failure to surrender the Smith jewels, ordered her immediate commitment to the penitentiary to serve the previously ordered 18-month sentence. Mary's outbursts and denials were unavailing. The distraught and desperate woman was delivered to the place of confinement.

The humble woman's commitment to the penitentiary stirred village sentiment, and prompted a move among the citizens for the petition of Mary's release. Mrs. Smith's loss of decorative adornment stood in sharp contrast to the deprivation that had fallen upon Mary Gilmore's family. Avon Lake citizens brought their petition before Judge Washburn decrying the suffering endured by Mary's now abandoned minor children. An older brother, who was employed as a well-digger, was only marginally successful in meeting the needs of his siblings, one of whom was suffering with tuberculosis and without needed care or medicine. Locals decried the situation as entirely inhumane.

Remembering the woman as hard-working and with no past transgressions, community sentiment against the heavy hand of wealth had mobilized a village against the disparity of consequences resulting from two poorly made decisions. Mary's crime had been confessed. But as one Avon Laker remarked to the press, if Mrs. Smith was foolish enough to carry her jewels in her stocking, then she ought to lose them.

Chapter 6

Green Gables

Sketch of John Gehring by Edith Newman

Undeterred by any fallout from economic disparity or the threat of a fickle lake, infiltrating Clevelanders continued seasonal migration to their summer homes. While all delighted in their Avon Lake country estates, perhaps none did so much as John Gehring. His striking shoreside estate was the venue for social events that frequently drew the notice of newspaper society pages.

John was the son of C. E. Gehring, an immigrant from Wurtenburg, Germany, who was part of a contingent of German brewers in Cleveland who developed family-owned businesses and distributed their beers and ales by horse-drawn wagon. The original Gehring Brewery, established in 1852, was located on Cleveland's west side, where the name "Gehring" street still survives. John Gehring joined his father's business, and ascended to its presidency in 1908.

John's first wife was Alvie Zangerle, sister of Cuyahoga County auditor John Zangerle. They were wed in a ceremony at the home of the bride's father in April 1887. The couple then left for a honeymoon trip to California as their Franklin Avenue home in Cleveland was being completed. Alvie's tenure as mistress of that stately manse was brought to an abrupt end by her death on January 25, 1890. According to Cuyahoga County death records, Alvie's cause of death at the age of 27 was pneumonia.[5]

Photo of headstone of Alvie Gehring taken at Riverside Cemetery in Cleveland, Ohio, courtesy of Karl Brunjes

---

[5] Cuyahoga County Record of Deaths also shows an entry for "Baby Gehring", stillborn on January 25, 1890, at the same address listed as Alvie's place of death, attended by the same physician, and buried in Riverside Cemetery, Cleveland, Ohio – the same burial location for Alvie Gehring.

Nine years following Alvie's death, Gehring had a country home built for himself along Avon Lake's shoreline near the Lake Shore Electric Railway's Stop 58.[6] The grand structure was the creation of Cleveland architect Frederick Baird, whose larger works included the 1902 Salvation Army Citadel on Erie Street and St. Theodosius Russian Orthodox Church on Starkweather.[7] Baird was the husband of Mamie Zangerle, sister of Gehring's deceased wife, Alvie.

In June of 1899, Gehring's new country estate was completed. A *Cleveland Plain Dealer* newspaper reporter disclosed that the home had finally been named. "Green Gables" was formally opened, and was christened with a party hosted by Gehring's mother and sister.

The event was a portent of festive occasions to follow. Though Gehring spent the inclement winter months in "bachelor's quarters" at Cleveland's Hollenden Hotel, he remained at Green Gables each year for as long as weather would allow. In January of 1900, a *Plain Dealer* writer following Gehring's trail remarked that the latter had been one of the last to leave the shore and return to The Hollenden. "Mr. Gehring loves his country home so well that he intends to spend his Saturdays and Sundays there all through the remainder of the winter. There is no dearth of company at Green Gables at any season" the reporter proclaimed.

---

[6] The address was later designated as 32972 Lake Road in Avon Lake, Ohio.

[7] St. Theodosius was the site of one of the scenes in the 1978 movie *The Deer Hunter*.

Complete with a stable and a cottage concealed from view by the Swiss-style main house, the Green Gables compound drew the attention of socialites with its parties, celebrations, and annual fall clambakes. The coveted invitations to Gehring's clambakes were hailed by society news pages as cleverly crafted bits of souvenir artistry, with one such invitation featuring various views of the glorious Green Gables estate.

Green Gables, Avon Lake home of John Gehring, built in 1898

Gehring's sense of humor was revealed to the public following newspaper coverage of his September 1906 clambake. At the event, he was "gifted" with ownership of the Hollenden's resident mutt, "Bum". The pooch was delivered to Green Gables in the hope that Gehring might rehabilitate the animal, his former owner lamenting that Bum was suffering from "obesity and gout, due to his high living in the city."

Gehring accepted the challenge. With the aid of his new owner, Bum distinguished himself by submission of a letter that was published in the *Plain Dealer* some six weeks later reporting on his new life at the shore. Directing his remarks to his former owner, Bum "wrote" that "John Gehring is not such a bad pal", and that the canine was indeed slimming down, though none too cheerfully.

Bum reported seeing a rat at Green Gables that was not worth pursuing, as it was "not any bigger than some of those mice we used to play with." The pooch grumbled that a couple times he had found himself in fear of catching a cold or "going into tuberculosis" at his new home. He then cut his letter short, complaining that "my paw's beginning to get tired."

*Sketch of Bum by
Edith Newman*

Two years later, Gehring retired from the brewing business, and in 1910, he took Mary Armstrong as his second bride. That, too, would prove to be a marriage of short duration. On November 4, 1913, at the age of 51, John Gehring died in Avon Lake at his much-loved Green Gables. The cause of his death, like Alvie's, was pneumonia.

Gehring monument in Riverside Cemetery,
Cleveland, Ohio. Photo courtesy of Karl Brunjes

Craig-Y-Nos

John Gehring's obituary remembered him not only for his presidency of the Gehring family brewery, but also for his involvement as an officer on the board of The Victor Oil Company, a business founded by his friend and Avon Lake summer neighbor, Franklyn Rosenzweig. Also sharing in the leadership of Victor Oil was Edwin ("E. S.") Griffiths. It was Griffiths, along with his wife, Margaret Rusk Griffiths, who became Green Gables' successor owners. A renowned Cleveland industrialist, Griffiths was founder and president of Cleveland Machine & Manufacturing Company, as well as interest-holder in several banks and other Cleveland manufacturing companies.

With the transfer of Green Gables' ownership also came a change in the beautiful lake shore house's name. When the Griffiths family took occupancy of the former Green Gables, they re-named the home "Craig-Y Nos". Most likely named for a Gothic-style castle in the Upper Swansea Valley in Wales, Griffiths was of Welsh descent, and was firmly attached to the culture and politics of his homeland.

One-time owner and occupant of the majestic Craig-Y-Nos Castle in Wales was world-famous opera star Adelina Patti. As Griffiths was himself an avid devotee of choral music, Ms. Patti's castle may have been the inspiration for the re-naming of Green Gables. Griffiths was both a vocalist and a conductor, and in 1923, he and a group of Cleveland businessmen financed a trip by the Orpheus Male Choir to compete at a music festival in South Wales. He continued his patronage of the group, as did his wife, Margaret, who was herself a composer and a graduate of the New England Conservatory of Music in Boston.

Griffiths was credited with inducing his personal friend and Britain's former Prime Minister, David Lloyd George, to include Cleveland in the latter's 1923 United States tour with his wife and daughter. Cleveland marked the occasion with a variety of celebrations as British and American flags hung from the fronts of hotels, offices and bank buildings in honor of Lloyd George's arrival.

Local Avon Lake legend suggests that Lloyd George stayed at Craig-Y-Nos during this historic visit. That Lloyd George enjoyed the private hospitality of the Griffiths is documented. Location of such hospitality, however, was not disclosed.

Craig-Y-Nos remained the summer home of Mr. and Mrs. Griffiths for another decade after the celebrated appearance of Lloyd George. The venue served as the site of entertainment for the Welsh Club, and for meetings of the Women's Board of Grace Hospital, an organization in which Margaret served as first president. In January of 1930, Edwin Griffiths died of heart failure at the age of 58 while vacationing in Miami Beach, Florida.

Sketch of E. S. Griffiths
by Edith Newman

Margaret was vigilant in preserving and honoring Edwin's memory following his death. She financed the construction of a chapel at the Old Stone Church in Cleveland as a memorial to her late husband. She also continued financial support of Edwin's beloved Orpheus Men's Chorus, which performed musical pieces for several years in his memory.

Margaret continued spending summers at Craig-Y-Nos for only a few more years. In July of 1933, she hosted a niece's wedding in the Craig-Y-Nos rose garden, but by spring of 1934, the home was listed for sale. Described as a "beautiful Swiss chateau" with a separate guest house and large garage containing servants' quarters, its advertisement detailed the estate as containing eight bedrooms, a 15 x 30 foot living room, cobblestone fireplace, and hardwood floors. Green Gables, turned Craig-Y-Nos, found its buyer, but became nameless with its third owner.

In May of 1934, Margaret Griffiths transferred ownership of Craig-Y-Nos to Robert Hildebrandt. After the transfer, there was no longer a name associated with the house. Robert's parents, Charles and Katherine, moved into the home with him that same year. Charles was a German immigrant who founded the Hildebrandt Provision Company in Cleveland in the late 1800's, a meat-processing business that specialized in sausages and smoked meats.

As a young woman, Katherine took an active part in the business by cooking meals for the employees, and later rose to the position of company Vice President. Charles and Katherine had two sons, and three daughters. Their son Robert assumed presidency of the family business upon Charles' retirement, with Charles continuing as chairman of the board of the company he had established.

Charles and Katherine's two daughters each married Pfahl brothers. Daughter Mathilda married John Pfahl, owner of the Pfahl Electric Company in Cleveland. In July of 1935, Robert Hildebrandt transferred property in Avon Lake to his sister Mathilda, and the Pfahls became the owners of a lakeshore home at 32990 Lake Road, adjacent to the former Green Gables. Mathilda entertained in style at her home (which was not given a name). Active in the Avon Lake Garden Club, her home was the meeting place for the organization on several occasions. One such meeting featured a lecture on Williamsburg flowers followed by a string trio performance with musicians from Baldwin-Wallace College, and another offered movies of Yellowstone followed by the musical offerings of a harpist.

Pfahl Home at 32990 Lake Road, Avon Lake, Ohio.
Photo by Sherry Spenzer

View from back porch of Pfahl home shortly before its demolition in 2014. Photo by Sherry Spenzer

Mathilda died September 27, 1944, leaving an estate valued at $248,298 to her husband and two daughters, Catherine (who married Dr. Orie Mazanec in 1948) and Rosemary (who married Joseph F. Duber in 1952). Mathilda's mother, Katherine Hildebrandt, died in 1947, and her father, Charles, died ten years later, both of them having passed away in the lake shore home. In an uncanny coincidence, a notice appeared in the *Plain Dealer* announcing that:

Due to the death of
MRS. KATHARINA HILDEBRANDT
Hildebrandt Provision Company
WILL BE CLOSED
TUESDAY, FEBRUARY 4

followed by a strikingly similar announcement ten years later:

Due to the death
of our founder
Charles R. Hildebrandt
The Hildebrandt Provision Company
will be closed
all day Monday, February 4, 1957

Robert Hildebrandt continued as president of the business after his father's death. He never married, and had been involved in the family business throughout his life, also serving as its vice president and secretary. Robert died on March 2, 1965, at the age of 71, in the Green Gables home.

The residence at 32990 Lake Road and the former Green Gables remained in the Duber family until October 2013, when both were sold to a buyer who had the residences demolished in the spring of 2014 for new construction, leaving only remnants of the once glorious country estate of John Gehring.

*The guest house and garage in 2014, final vestiges of the former Green
Gables country estate. Photos by Sherry Spenzer*

Chapter 7

The Folger House

Only one lake shore summer home has endured – the Folger house, built in 1902 and located northwest of intersecting Avon Belden and Lake Roads, and west of Avon Point. Its original owner, Thomas Folger, was born February 14, 1842, in Wadsworth, Ohio, to Henry and Eliza Ingersoll Folger. Preceded by generations of enterprising men, Thomas' grandfather (also named Thomas) was a successful whaling boat captain, and his uncle, Charles Folger, served as Secretary of the United States Treasury under Presidents Arthur and Garfield.

As a youth of nineteen, Thomas and three of his boyhood friends from Wadsworth enlisted in Company H of the 29th OVI when the Civil War erupted. Thomas served nearly four years in the war, spending much of his time in active battle, including the battles of Gettysburg, Chancellorsville, and Peter's Mountain.[8] He culminated his years of service by accompanying Sherman in the March to the Sea. During his term of service, he sustained a hip injury, leaving him with a slight but permanent limp. Thomas ultimately achieved the rank of First Lieutenant, and was honorably discharged in July 1865.

---

[8] Various sources are at odds regarding Folger's participation in Second Bull Run and his ascent to the rank of Captain. While The *Cleveland Leader* newspaper of July 25, 1865 announced Folger's elevation to rank of Captain, such report is not supported by the Official Roster of the State of Ohio in the War of the Rebellion or the National Park Service's Civil War database, both of which show him as a First Lieutenant at time of discharge.

Following his military service, Thomas Folger settled in Cleveland, and in May of 1867 he married Della Beswick. His parents came to Cleveland to join them, and the extended family shared a home. Thomas and Della's first child, Anna, was born in 1869. Two more daughters were born to Thomas and Della in Cleveland - Josephine in 1872, and Ida in 1874. Thomas and Henry had partnered for several years in Folger, Willard & Co., a Cleveland commercial merchant establishment.

Their retailing activities took a new direction when Henry purchased 155 acres along the lake shore in Avon Lake, and Della and Eliza purchased 63 acres in 1875, a portion of which was already a producing vineyard. Thomas and Henry were rewarded with success in their cultivation of grapes, with concords being the primary crop. The extended Folger family had taken occupancy of an older home at their vineyard by 1875, and their youngest daughter, Jean, was born in 1879. Daughter Josephine later described their first lake shore home as a "strange old house" that had originally served as a stagecoach inn.

In 1882, the Folger family established a primary residence at East Second Street in Elyria, Ohio, where more educational and social opportunities were available to their daughters, and where Thomas found himself drawn to politics. The family continued to spend seasonable months at their lake shore home, where Thomas built a reputation as a knowledgeable and successful viticulturist. He later became founder and longtime manager of the Grape Growers' Association, an organization that served to protect the pricing and distribution of grapes harvested in the north central Ohio area.

In August of 1883, the first Folger lake shore home made news when Charles Folger, then Secretary of the Treasury under President Arthur, visited his brother Henry at the summer estate. Such was the last meeting of the brothers, as Henry died at Thomas' Elyria residence on November 29, 1883. The Folgers were twice struck by loss that year, as daughter Ida had died in January of 1883 of internal injuries sustained in a sledding accident.

Following Folger's relocation of his primary residence to Elyria came an increased involvement in local politics. An active Democrat in a Republican-dominated city, Folger served in Elyria as a councilman while maintaining his involvement in grape retailing as manager of the Lorain County Grape Growers' Shipping Association. The family continued their seasonal pilgrimages to the lake shore home, where Della and her daughters frequently entertained.

On June 20, 1895, Folger gave his eldest daughter, Anna, in marriage to Charles Braman, who later became president of the Savings Deposit Bank and Trust Company in Elyria. That wedding was quickly followed by the nuptials of daughter Josephine, who wed Dr. Charles Cushing on December 4, 1895 at the Folger Elyria residence.

Two of the Folger daughters - Anna Folger, third from left, and Josephine Folger, third from right – in the "Sisters Club". Photo courtesy of Heritage Avon Lake

In February 1896, Folger became involved in the Elyria banking business, and was elected one of the directors of the Penfield Avenue Savings Bank. His primary focus, however, continued to be the grape industry, and the profitable distribution of its harvested fruit. In July of 1899, the *Cleveland Leader* newspaper questioned the continuing success of the grape growers' exchange, suggesting that the expected dissolution of the Northern Ohio Grape Association would leave each grower to fend for himself in the market. A sharp responsive letter to that paper explained that the association had not dissolved, but had consolidated with managers of five independent companies – Folger being the representative of one of those – to ensure "a mutual daily understanding in regard to prices, and a more even distribution of the sales, thereby avoiding the overstocking of any one market during the rush of the season".

On June 14, 1900, Folger escorted his last daughter down the aisle as she exchanged vows with Arthur Pettibone, an "official of the Bessemer Steamship Co." By 1901, all three daughters and their spouses were regular summer visitors at the original Folger lake shore home, and in September 1901, an article in the *Elyria Reporter* announced that a new thirty-room residence was to be erected on the Folger property for the use of the increased family, with sons-in-law Braman, Cushing, and Pettibone all being interested in the construction. The home was scheduled to be completed before summer of 1902.

By June 26, 1902, the extended Folger family was enjoying their new summer residence, but with one incident of minor inconvenience to Thomas Folger. On August 18, 1902, Folger had made a solo return trip to his Elyria home. Lights in the home drew the attention of neighbors, who presumed him to be at the lake shore with his family. Police were called, the home was surrounded by a throng of watching neighbors, and a search of the premises was made. Police officers found an unsuspecting Folger asleep on the second floor of his home, all to the amusement of the gathered public.

In March 1903, Folger's avid support of the Democratic Party resulted in his nomination for mayor of Elyria. Facing an uphill battle in a Republican-dominated city, Folger's challenger was the incumbent Dr. Reefy. In an election billed by the *Elyria Reporter* newspaper as "a stinging rebuke" of Mayor Reefy and the manner of his nomination by the Republican Party, Folger won the office of mayor of Elyria in April 1903 by 147 votes. The *Elyria Republican* newspaper softened the announcement of victory by characterizing Folger as "a gentleman, a capable business man, and experienced in Elyria's public affairs" who was expected to make a good mayor.

Folger commenced his term in April 1903, his service in presiding over mayor's court occupying much of his official time. His dispositions of the many cases before him revealed the character of Thomas Folger. He demonstrated firmness, a propensity for second chances, and an intolerance toward abuse or neglect of families and animals.

Folger's first case in mayor's court resulted in imposition of a fine for violation of Sunday liquor sales, followed by a series of cases involving "tramps" who were routinely arrested and brought from the streets to mayor's court. Folger had limited tolerance for the freeloaders who invaded the city, and was prompt to order them to work on the "street gangs" consigned to city improvement tasks. One feisty defendant warned that he was going to sue Folger for false imprisonment, to which Folger reportedly to said "That's all right – you run along and tend to your sweeping. After you get through you can sue as much as you want to", the sweeping task having been the sentence imposed in the case.

The newly installed mayor assured the citizenry that he would preserve Elyria's reputation as "an undesirable port for tramps to steer". Compassion, however, trumped such determination when a vagrant, who was also an old soldier, appeared before Folger. The mayor gave the elderly man thirty minutes to get out of town – and then provided the hapless vagabond ten cents to do so.

Folger's patience wore thin, though, when he provided another homeless defendant with sufficient funds to make his way to Lorain to pursue employment. The deceitful recipient of Folger's beneficence chose instead to spend the money on alcohol. The result was an order to get out of town within thirty minutes, and with no assistance to the banished bamboozler.

Folger showed no tolerance in cases of animal abuse, ordering fines and days on the street gang to those who were found to have whipped, kicked, or starved their horses. Animal theft was equally offensive to Folger, who issued stiff penalties and "street gang" sentences to one defendant who stole a litter of pups, and to another who stole a woman's pet poodle. Most abhorrent to Folger, however, were men who abandoned or failed to support their wives and children. Those men could count on time in the workhouse, but could expect parole upon giving convincing assurance that if released, their families would be properly provided for.

Folger occasionally revealed a lighter side. In one instance, he let a group of skinny-dipping boys off with a warning regarding proper swim attire. In another, he allowed a penniless vaudeville performer charged with intoxication to satisfy his fine by performing a song and dance routine for the court and staff's amusement.

Folger's popularity with the people and his commitment to public service did not go unnoticed in upper levels of government. In September 1903, his party wanted to nominate him as a candidate for State Senator. Folger declined, but did accept the governor's appointment to a prison reform congress in Kentucky, an issue in which Folger had a keen interest.

The days of presiding over mayor's court had evidently begun to test his honor's patience, as the local paper carried a story in 1905 on Folger's "magic chair" lecture as given to one defendant. The man had been charged with intoxication. He solicited no compassion from Folger with his pitiful excuses for the misuse of his family's funds on intoxicants.

Folger's ensuing lecture to the defendant was steeped in sarcasm. "That's the magic chair and everyone who sits in it is honest and sincere", Folger told the man occupying the defendant's seat. "You are sitting in a charmed chair just where hundreds of others have sat and it makes you for the time very repentant, very sorrowful, very desirous of going and sinning no more. The time to remember your responsibility is before you drink."

The man then attempted to bargain with Folger, asking him for a ticket to Cleveland. The defendant assured the judge that once he arrived at his intended destination, friends would provide him money to pay his fine. The man promised that he would then mail the funds to the court. Having heard more than enough from the man, Folger simply ordered him transported to jail.

Throughout his mayoral tenure, Folger continued his regular treks to his Avon Point country home, and remained actively involved with the grape growers association. As his term drew to conclusion, he first announced his intent to seek re-election. Within months of that announcement, and following some friction within the Democratic Party, Folger withdrew from the race, and instead announced his retirement, citing ill health as his motivation for withdrawing from public service.

Retirement was hardly on Folger's horizon, though, as he immediately involved himself with some Cleveland businessmen in a plan to build a distillery on several acres of his Avon Point property. Folger's plan was to dispose of refuse grapes and other unsaleable fruits and vegetables by distilling them into denatured alcohol. Much of the castoff produce for distillation would be grapes that spoiled during delays in distribution. The resulting product could then be used as fuel.

The distillery never materialized, but two years later, Folger was lured by the return to public life. He was nominated as mayoral candidate for a second term of office in August 1909. The candidacy was short-lived, however, as Folger died of a heart attack in his Avon Point home at the age of 67 on October 13, 1909.

The family continued reunions at the summer home until the time of Della Folger's death in 1922. The Folger property ultimately came into the hands of H. G. Barker, who sold it to the Village of Avon Lake in 1926. Since that time, the Folger dwelling has housed various city offices, including village clerk's office, council chambers, and the municipal court. It was the meeting place of American Legion Post 211 when the group first organized. It functioned as a teen center in the 1940's and 1950's, housed several groundskeepers and their families, and a mayor's office. In 1988, it became Veterans Park Hall. In 2002, an organization, formed under the name of Avon Lake Landmark Preservation Society, leased the home, and painstakingly devoted itself to the care, renovation, and preservation of the house and its history. In 2016, that task was assumed by Heritage Avon Lake, which continues the effort today.

The Folger home, Avon Lake, built in 1902.
Photo courtesy of Heritage Avon Lake

Della Folger with grand-daughter Josephine at left, Thomas Folger at right. Photos courtesy of Heritage Avon Lake

Chapter 8

Beach Park Ballyhoo

Built in 1897, Avon Lake's renowned Beach Park resort drew crowds each summer from 1898 until 1922, when sale of the property to Cleveland Electric Illuminating Company was negotiated. The alluring recreation site was constructed primarily with Lake Shore Electric Railway funds, whose profits were fortified by the fares of passengers travelling from both east and west to the vacation spot. The park featured a large pavilion and dance hall, a merry-go-round (the first one having become the unfortunate casualty of a storm in 1901), a midway, boating, fishing, bathing, billiards, baseball, bowling, and "funny laughing mirrors". Beach Park boldly pronounced its baseball grounds the best in Lorain County.

Beach Park in 1913. Post Card courtesy of Bernadette Hisey

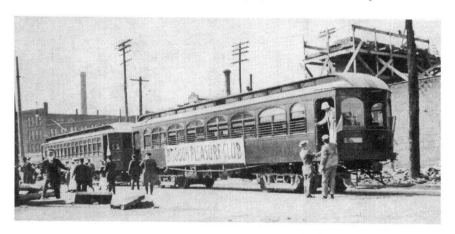

The park drew Sunday school class picnics, church bazaars, family reunions, and folks in search of a fresh fish dinner. A 1907 Avon Farmers' Picnic sought to entice attendees with the assurance of every kind of race or contest ever offered, promising the prize of a greased pig to the one skilled enough to catch it. Local 235 - "Lorain County's Master Horse Shoeers"- and journeymen, invaded the grounds with families in tow for a day of picnicking and games. Organized baseball teams competed for bragging rights, and would issue challenges to one another through the newspapers. Requests would appear in such form as:

> "The Leaders would like to play the V.P.C.'s Sunday, July 10, at Avon Beach. Answer through this paper."[9]

Beach Park dance hall with bowling alley to the right.
Photo Courtesy of Thomas J. Patton

---

[9] From *The Cleveland Leader* (Cleveland, Ohio), June 28, 1904, p. 9.

Swimmers and boaters were attracted to the park's shore, a seasonal escape with no dearth of summer fun. A keenly successful endeavor, Beach Park was hailed as one of the most beautiful of the suburban resorts of Ohio. Offering respite from the mundanity of crowded urban life, Avon Lake beckoned increasing numbers of Clevelanders with the lure of sandy beaches and cooling summer breezes. In April of 1901, Beach Park boasted management by W.T. and O.F.H. Kaserman, billed as "well-known dancing masters of the West Side". This evolving urban escape was irresistible during an era when city dwellers hungered for recreational activity and outdoor amusement, as Beach Park offered both.

Summer fun at Beach Park. Photo courtesy of Bernadette Hisey

The park's popularity expanded as retail, professional, and commercial establishments hosted employee picnics on the grounds. The shoreline's summertime retreat served as gathering place for such business organizations as the Ohio Wine and Spirit Association, The West Side Merchants Association, the Lorain County and Cuyahoga County physicians, and the Ohio Retail Druggists Association. The civic minded gathered at Beach Park in 1903 for the Elks September clambake, and lapping waves along the shore competed with wailing bagpipes as the Blue Bell Lodge hosted lively Scottish dances and a soccer match in 1913.

The Telling Bros. ice cream manufacturers feted 400 employees with a chicken dinner and an inviting program of athletic contests. The West Side Master Plumbers similarly hosted a variety of athletic competitions, games, and dancing, and over 600 employees of the Higbee Company store required use of nine special Lake Shore Electric Railway cars to make their way to a Beach Park outing that featured a baseball game against the Press teams, followed by dinner and dancing.

Bath house along shore at Beach Park.
Photo courtesy of Thomas J. Patton

Beach Park picnic and games in 1917.
Photo courtesy of Thomas J. Patton

All events were, of course, accessible by Lake Shore Electric's railway, with special event cars being frequently provided. In 1910, Beach Park's advertisements sought to attract an elite patronage with the claim that "we cater to the better class – are you one of them?"

Also known as Avon Beach Park, this thriving mecca of entertainment delights stretched nearly 30 acres along Lake Erie's shore. Its pavilion and dance hall offered such amenities as electric lights, hot and cold water, steam heat, and a large open fireplace for winter parties. A caterer on site specialized in chicken dinners. One advertisement enticed dancers with the following:

> "For those that seek enjoyment in dancing – we have added an expensive and wonderful feature in the form of an electric scenic effect – which gives the impression that you are dancing in a Real Snowstorm – changing to rain and through the mist at Niagara Falls – you surely will marvel at this wonderful attraction."

Dance Hall at Beach Park. Photo courtesy of Thomas J. Patton

Women sporting Beach Park sashes. Photo courtesy of Bernadette Hisey

While the park dazzled with manicured flower beds, shade trees, and a stunning lake view by day, Beach Park's night life harbored a dark side that distressed the locals and stirred political action. On August 31, 1899, an Elyria newspaper recounted an attack on a local man as he departed Beach Park premises on a Sunday night. The unfortunate patron was assaulted and cut with a sharp object, sustaining serious injury.

The newspaper harshly criticized Beach Park as having degenerated into "a pretty rough place", particularly on Sunday nights, attracting "thugs and bad characters for miles around". Beach Park's reputation was made even more questionable by its ownership of two of the six saloons operating in the combined Avon and Beach Park areas, prompting locals to undertake their own attack on the park's disruption of community peace.

As early as 1894, neighboring Avon held a local option vote, which left the "wets" victorious and the "drys" undeterred. Women of longstanding Avon Lake pedigree, including Mrs. Ida Jaycox (of Jaycox Road connection) and Mrs. Orlando Moore (of Moore Road connection) hosted meetings of the Women's Christian Temperance Union (WCTU) and garnered support for Avon Lake's own local option elections. Arguments advanced by opponents of the efforts as published by one Cleveland newspaper did little to dissuade the temperance folks, making such claims as:

> "... if passed, [the local option ordinance] will drive people to drink in back and upstairs rooms. People are made drunkards because of certain laws. Temperance people are making whisky drinkers instead of beer drinkers of the American people. With liberal laws people will drink beer, and a beer drinker is not a drunkard; it's the whisky drinker that is."

Undaunted by the protestations of saloon supporters, the temperance ladies become even more impassioned. In May of 1900, Avon Lake was the site of the County WCTU's semi-annual convention, where their stated purpose was twofold: closing local saloons, and securing the ballot for women. They characterized their battle as "the saloon against the home".

By March 1903, a local Anti-Saloon League was also established in Avon Lake. Sufficient signatures were collected, and a special election was set to determine whether saloons in Avon and Avon Lake would be closed. A Cleveland newspaper captioned the election story "Saloon Brawl May 'Dry' Avon", and reported that "the fight is one of the most complicated in which the Anti-Saloon league of the Cleveland district has taken a hand". The ballot "brawl" was ostensibly instigated in part by the complaints of local farmers whose sons and daughters were idling away their Sundays at Beach Park, dancing until late at night, spending their money, and wasting their time. Beach Park was alleged to be dispensing "fizz" - identified by those knowledgeable as being a lager beer – and operating slot machines where young men were "losing much money".

Other Avon Lake citizens despaired of two saloons located at Beach Park, which they blamed for multiple inconveniences and property value decline. Concerning Beach Park, Cleveland's *Plain Dealer* reported that:

" . . . during the summer months great crowds from Lorain and Cleveland are wont to visit the park pavilion, making too much noise to suit citizens living near. On account of the sale of liquor, it is said, property in the immediate neighborhood cannot be readily disposed of."

Opposing the curtailment of saloon operations was, according to the press, the Lake Shore Electric Railway, who had allegedly ordered its employees residing in the Beach Park "colony" to vote "wet".

The prospect of a dry town was fraught with potential for a great loss of revenue to the Railway that ran cars filled with thirsty revelers to Beach Park. A dry town would further pose a threat to continued employment of Lake Shore Electric Railway workers, who were thus induced to "vote wet". An opposing voice, which made its way into newsprint, proclaimed that the upcoming vote would decide whether Avon Lake would "take her place among the respectable townships of Lorain County", or would "continue to bear her present unsavory reputation."

Reputation gave way to recreation, and the option was defeated. On March 26, 1903, the *Plain Dealer* newspaper announced that "The resort known as Beach Park may continue to sell liquor". Temperance workers were offered some consolation in the fact that defeat on this occasion was by a much smaller margin than that suffered at a local option election held three years prior. The great offender, however – Beach Park – was left to thrive despite the annoyances to locals wrought by Lorain and Cleveland invaders and the attendant provocations of intoxicants.

At least one resident was assuaged in his concern about French Creek in Avon following their local option defeat, but was not so charitable in his assessment of Beach Park. In a letter published by the *Plain Dealer*, Rev. Father A. B. Stuber of the Avon Catholic Church wrote:

> "The saloon keepers of French Creek have promised to be good hereafter, and if they will fulfill their promise the election will have had a good effect. It may take the full severity of the law to reform Beach Park, which is situated four to five miles from French Creek and East Avon."

Reform, however, was not yet to be, and controversy over the alcohol issue was about to heat up from "simmer" to "boil".

Chapter 9

Unhinged at Beach Park

Beach Park locals were troubled by more than just the chaos of invading picnickers, revelers, and saloon patrons. In 1905, one of their own residents engaged in a bizarre rampage against the townspeople that left them terrorized. Peter Pitts, a 22-year-old farmer's son, had begun displaying "signs of insanity." As his bizarre behavior escalated, he grew increasingly violent, firing random shots at unsuspecting neighbors.

He was bold in his assaults, trespassing into the homes of his intended victims at night and shooting at them with a pistol. In the course of one evening, he shot at a young woman as she was driving her cows home, ambushed Dr. Pipes twice while the latter was making house calls, and fired shots at the Beach Park dance hall, inciting panic amongst the dancers.

For days citizens hid in their homes from the town terror. Local constables refused to become involved in Pitts' search and capture. County Sheriff Salsbury was thus forced into action, but he was not without aid.

Posses of several hundred farmers and deputies all joined the effort to halt Pitts. The latter managed to elude his pursuers at the commencement of the campaign, thus affording him sufficient time to destroy a large farmhouse by piling bundles of straw against the building and then setting the bundles on fire. The unsuspecting family fled their home in their night clothes as it was consumed by flames, with Pitts shooting at them as they ran, striking one young woman in the leg.

Pitts continued with his campaign of destruction by piling railroad ties on the Lake Shore Electric Railway track, apparently with the intention of causing a wreck. The railway operator was able, however, to bring the cars to a halt before striking the barricade. Early the following morning, Pitts concluded his work by robbing a farmer of his watch, but on this occasion allowed the latter to escape without shooting him.

Fortunately for the townspeople, Pitts had a remarkably poor aim, and no deaths resulted. His reign of terror, however, continued for three days, with deputies fearful that Pitts was heading for Lorain to continue his destruction. The posses chased Pitts from his hiding places and then flushed him from the home of a relative. Pitts fled and "tore through the underbrush and woods, over fields and vineyards like one possessed for a mile and a half" according to the report of one local newspaper.

Finally, the posse's prey weakened. Rather than be taken captive, Pitts turned his pistol on himself and ended his own life. He was found by deputies in a field between Case Road and Stoney Ridge Road south of French Creek Village about an hour after the suicide. Examination was made by the coroner, and the body was taken to the home of the man's parents in Beach Park.

The deceased was described by the *Canton Repository* newspaper as being "young, powerfully built, intelligent." It was because of these attributes, claimed the *Repository*, that Pitts, upon turning maniacal, was "more dangerous than an ordinary man would have been under the same circumstances". The subject was reported to have been "in the best of health" up to a week before his rampage, with his aberrant behavior being attributed to sudden insanity resulting from "a most dangerous form of dementia".

One report of his death asserted that Pitts was "found with four bullet holes in his chest", and that it was necessary for him to reload his pistol after two of the shots had been fired. The act was claimed to be evidence of a "superhuman strength with which [Pitts'] crazed condition had temporarily possessed him".

Grave of Peter Pitts in St. Mary's Cemetery, Avon, Ohio. Photo by Sherry Spenzer

Less than two months after Pitts' death, a local newspaper reported that Peter's elderly aunt, Emma Pitts, was adjudicated insane by the Lorain County Probate Court following her copycat attempt to shoot Dr. Pipes. Another article attributed her loss of sanity to her nephew's suicide, claiming the woman's already weak mind had become "unhinged" by the event. Emma had allegedly pronounced that it was necessary for her to kill someone, as God demanded a sacrifice, she having "received the command personally". Emma was committed to a state asylum in October 1905, and died there in May of the following year.

The curse continued to haunt the Pitts family as Peter's uncle, Mathias Pitts, was adjudicated insane in 1906, and again in 1910. Mathias prompted the second adjudication when he armed himself with clubs and a corn knife, claiming to be a victim of some unspecified persecution. A warrant was issued for the man's arrest and commitment, and a newspaper account of Mathias' 1910 insanity adjudication made no ridicule of County Sheriff Ward's stated contention that insanity cases, like fires, came three in succession.

Sheriff Ward sold the Pitts family short, however, as the same article recounting Mathias' last episode recalled a much earlier insanity adjudication within the same family. Peter's aunt and Mathias' sister, Margaret "Maggie" Pitts of Avon Lake residence, had been ruled insane and committed to the Newburg Asylum in Cleveland in 1881. She was the victim of a tragic fire that ravaged that facility in October 1887. Rendered nearly unrecognizable by the severity of her burns, Maggie was only 33 years old at the time of her death, and a subsequent news article reported that no-one had come to claim the dead woman's body.

Four years following the last Pitts insanity declaration, Beach Park watched as a popular attraction turned into another tragedy. An amusement draw for the park from as early as 1910, onlookers would gather along the shore to watch hot air balloon ascensions. Ads beckoned the curious to "follow the crowd" to Beach Park and observe as skilled aeronauts were carried aloft by hot air balloons, then dropped by parachute with Lake Erie as the spectacular backdrop.

On Sunday, May 24, 1914, a crowd of 5,000 spectators gathered at Beach Park to watch 22-year-old William Warner of Piqua, Ohio, execute the hot air balloon stunt. With his young bride of five months amongst the onlookers, the balloon was caught by a wind and carried out over Lake Erie. Horrified observers stood helpless as Warner and his parachute fell 1,000 feet into the water below.

The widow stayed with Beach Park friends as a week-long search was made for the body. A lifesaving crew from Lorain joined the effort, but days passed without recovery of any remains. Speculation was that the body had been pinned to the lake bottom by the heavy parachute.

Finally, on June 1, 1914, William's hometown newspaper, the *Piqua Daily Call*, reported that the young aeronaut's body had been found. His remains were shipped to his grieving father in Piqua. His widow's meager consolation came as an order by the state industrial commission that William's employer pay her the sum of $1,500, in bi-weekly installments of $10 each, for the loss of her husband.

Chapter 10

The Demise of Beach Park

Although Beach Park had managed to survive local option controversy, the gunfire of a crazed man, and a tragic air balloon spectacle, the legendary resort was facing its demise. In 1923, the Cleveland Illuminating Company purchased Beach Park and its power plant. By March of 1924, CEI announced its plans to construct a new plant at the site, with a 132,000-volt transmission line at a cost of $30,000,000. The project was hailed as one of the five biggest electricity generating stations in America using steam power, with all of those stations located in or near Cleveland, Detroit, and Chicago.

Avon Lake landowners used the power plant hype to market their property, contending that once CEI construction commenced, housing site costs would escalate. Farmers faced court hearings as CEI initiated eminent domain proceedings for high tension lines, and disputes arose over the matter of adequate compensation.

Beach Park Power Plant c. 1913. Photo courtesy of Thomas J. Patton

Progress was not to be thwarted. Construction proceeded in March of 1925 after courts had been kept busy deciding the fair value of appropriated farmlands and determining the amounts of monetary judgments to be awarded to inconvenienced farmers. The plant boasted future growth that would eventually contribute 400,000 horsepower over a super-power system that would service four states. It enthusiastically predicted favorable industrial expansion as a result of the additional power, and forecasted an increase in population being drawn to the area with the lure of an ease in labor. CEI made public its hope to lay claim to being the largest steam generating plant in the world.

Shrewd real estate sales companies did not miss the opportunity to promote land sales in Avon Lake. With the promise of the development of "Dreamland Beach" to be constructed just east of the new power plant, the Gayitch Realty Company of Cleveland offered the curious a chance to see and consider "the Sensation of 1925". In May of that year, promoters enticed the curious with "unusual amusement and entertainment", a free ride by the Lake Shore Electric Railway car to the site, and a free band concert. At 3:00 p.m., attendees would be treated to airplane stunts, free refreshments, and souvenirs of the event. The formal opening of the development was to be marked by the dropping of a huge golden key from an airplane.

The following month, another festively-fused event was promoted by Gayitch Realty whereby interested Clevelanders could attend a band concert at Public Square at 12:30 p.m., then meet at Marshall's Drug Store upon conclusion of the concert, and be transported by private automobile to Avon Lake to view the new power plant. An educational trip, music, and refreshments were promised, as was the prospect of the option to purchase a future home site at "$650 up".

The CEI hype was capped on August 4, 1926 at noon at a special public inauguration service. With press on hand to cover the event, the switch was flipped at Avon Lake's illustrious new energy plant by the renowned Charles F. Brush, the man who had perfected arc lighting and invented street lighting. With that history-making gesture, the power plant was formally installed, Avon Lake was illuminated, and the once celebrated Beach Park was no more than a dimming memory.

Present view of illuminating plant. Photo by Connor Beach

Chapter 11

1920's Roar on the Shore

In January of 1920, the battle between "wets" and "drys" had taken a new twist. With the 18th Amendment to the U.S. Constitution, the introduction of "Prohibition" criminalized the manufacture, sale, or transportation of intoxicating liquors for other than medicinal use. Rather than deter the consumption of alcohol, Prohibition simply fueled a new, illicit industry.

A new breed of scofflaws emerged, and as the 1920's roared, so did the shores of Avon Lake. "Rum runners" matched wits and skill with enforcement agents and the Coast Guard as alcohol was illegally transported from Canada to points along Lake Erie's southern shore. The ill-gotten goods - referred to generically as "rum" – were then distributed to eager retailers. Establishments serving alcohol relied on buzzers hidden under bars and window sills, false walls, and peepholes in doors to skirt detection.

Restaurants, ice cream stores, candy shops, and dry cleaners all served as fronts for alcohol sales. "Districts" were established amongst rum-runners, and encroachment into neighboring territories was not tolerated. Adherence to pricing "standards" was expected.

While consumers simply side-stepped the law to have their thirst for alcohol quenched, one Avon Lake physician took a more aggressive stance and voiced his protest to the Medical Society and the press in an attempt to remedy the imposition that Prohibition placed upon doctors. Practitioners could no longer provide patients with alcohol to palliate a variety of medical conditions, but could only write prescriptions to be filled by pharmacists in limited quantities. Dr. F. M. McMechan, an Avon Lake practitioner, cited the treatment of diphtheria in support of his opposition to such medical infringement, using as an example the argument that whiskey was the antidote at certain stages of diphtheria.

McMechan contended that a four-year-old child could be given a quart of whiskey over a 24-hour period without intoxicating effects, "the poison of the liquor and the disease neutralizing each other". The physician protested that he would be left having to buy liquor of questionable quality from bootleggers for medical treatment. Prohibition law exemptions were not adopted as a result of McMechan's efforts, the wisdom of administering a quart of whiskey to a young child perhaps being of greater concern.

Retailers of the forbidden spirits were sometimes the manufacturers as well. One local, the operator of a "soft drink parlor" in Cleveland, was arrested and fined following the discovery of 2,500 gallons of wine stored in his Avon Lake home. Mayor's court kept Avon Lake's Mayor Howard Walker busy as he issued fines and jail sentences to violators, including a gathering of guests who had assembled at an Avon Lake "cottage party" where they "imbibed until achieving intoxication".

The more active trade, however, was off Erie's shore. Scrutiny of lake craft activity and the arrest of a pair of rum-runners off Avon Lake's shores led to local law enforcement's declaration of discovery of a Lorain-Cleveland "booze route". Avon Point – already renowned for its catastrophic events – was particularly active with the illicit trade.

The danger wrought by violent storms off Avon Point was rapidly being rivaled by the treachery of night-time rum-running activity. The same scenic shores that beckoned picnickers and bathers by day metamorphosed into a maelstrom of offshore illegal activity by night.

The area drew the focus of news media on September 18, 1924, when it was discovered that prominent Clevelanders Patience and Martin Thayer were missing from their abandoned yacht, the Wing and Wing. Initial theory was that the couple's craft had become disabled at Avon Point, and that the Thayers then sought shore by tender.

Discovery of a capsized rowboat suggested a tragic outcome. Follow-up reports, however, stirred other speculation after the bodies were washed ashore west of Avon Point, with one newspaper laying suspicion on "rum pirates". A federal investigation was launched, and another newspaper exposed the theory that the Thayers had been the target of rum-runners after loaning their yacht to federal authorities in undercover rum-running busts.

The local war on booze was expanded to include an assault on gambling, a companion diversion in those clandestine sites of underworld entertainment where peepholes and passwords were used to screen prospective patrons. Rumors of "protection money" extorted from proprietors of such establishments were fueled by repeated incidents of unexplained property destruction. The Mob's high profile big-city control of alcohol distribution set the tone for local operations, and gangland style of enforcement of underworld codes reached even the venues of Avon Lake. "Protected" businesses would continue to function, but those that went "uninsured" could be abruptly shut down by disastrous misfortune. Avon Lake's Black Whale Inn on Lake Road at Stop 58[10] of the Lake Shore Electric Railway may have experienced such a "lapse" in its coverage.

Ad for the Black Whale Inn from 1923 Avon Lake School Fair program. Courtesy Avon Lake Public Library

---

[10] Stop 58 is at the general location of the present Beachwood Road in Avon Lake.

In mid-March of 1926, a neighbor discovered flames breaking into the first floor of the former Black Whale Inn from its basement. The inn, which had alternately served as a private residence, was destroyed by the blaze. Also consumed by the fire was an unoccupied neighboring home known to locals as the D.H. Hanna house.

Both properties were owned by the same man, who was residing in Cleveland when the destruction occurred. Neighbors called for the additional assistance of the Lorain Fire Department. The latter declined to respond or render aid.

Authorities were later reportedly in search of a "firebug", the cause of the Black Whale's destruction having been deemed of suspicious nature, it being the fourth fire to strike neighboring cities in two days. All had occurred within miles of each other, with blazes originating in the basements, and all were ruled casualties of incendiarism. The demise of the Black Whale Inn and the Hannah house may have prompted investigation of arson, but the threat of investigation was no deterrent to arsonists as road houses remained frequent targets.

One of Avon Lake's tributes to the 1920's new style of music and dance that offered a welcome diversion to a war-weary nation was the celebrated Lake Road Inn – a popular road house near the lake's shore. Born of the new passion for syncopated rhythms and energetic dance styles, Lake Road Inn was a thriving entertainment spot. It drew big names in entertainment and throngs of patrons, then disappeared in a shroud of mystery.

Located at "Stop 41" - the Lakeshore Electric Railway Stop that was located in the expanse between Cove Avenue and Highland just west of the Lorain and Cuyahoga County border - the inn proclaimed itself one of the area's finest. It boasted a 5,000-square-foot dance floor, with a dining room capacity of 400. Lake Road Inn offered its patrons chicken, steak, or fish dinners for $2.50 a plate, and dancing from 6:00 p.m. until midnight. Non-diners could dance for a cover charge of 50 cents. The inn opened its season in spring, and remained open through mid-fall.

Lake Road Inn's entertainment featured such rising stars as Guy Lombardo and The Royal Canadians, who later became legendary as a dance band. The inn was also a venue for acclaimed singer/comedienne Sophie Tucker, and for Herb Weidoeft and his orchestra, whose performances promised "scintillating music" to patrons for their dancing pleasure. As the music grew more scintillating, so did Lake Road Inn's reputation. A raid was attempted at the inn on the night of June 12, 1926, but plans were leaked to news reporters in advance of the event. A gathering of reporters outside of the inn drew the attention of its proprietor, who was able to thwart the efforts of law enforcement. On July 7, 1926, however, a second raid was successfully conducted, with $2,500 in gambling equipment seized from a targeted "gambling house" located in close proximity to the inn.

Remnant of Lake Road Inn. Photo courtesy of Avon Lake Public Library, donated by Barney Klement

Twenty-three arrests resulted, with those arraigned described in a local newspaper as all "well bred men". In early July of 1926, rumors of the inn's imminent closing had been circulating. Lake Road Inn did in fact close its doors with the raid, and on October 14, 1926, the celebrated "rendezvous of northern Ohio dancers and diners" had burned to the ground. The estimated loss was $175,000. While origin of the blaze was unknown, it did not escape notice by news reporters that the inn's loss added "another to the series of mysterious blazes which have been reported along the lake road between Lorain and Cleveland during the last year".

Blossom Heath, an inn at Rocky River, followed as an incendiary casualty. It and Lake Road Inn had been vaunted as "two of the most important summer road houses" by one Cleveland newspaper. Blossom Heath was burned to the ground on May 9, 1927. Its proprietor told one reporter he had been warned that "they'll get you next", but refused to name any suspects.

Speculation was aroused. Some pointed fingers at the Mafia. Some blamed rival road house operators. The case of Lake Road Inn's destruction was never solved, no arson charges were ever brought, and no perpetrators were ever identified.

While local road houses became casualties of unsolved crime, one Avon Lake resident was prospering in production and – apparently – distribution of illegal alcohol. In a raid conducted in August of 1927 on the "mansion" of Neil Radell at Lake Shore Electric's Stop 55[11], Lorain County Sheriff O. E. Rankin and sixteen deputies hit the jackpot. The basement of Radell's home was furnished with tables suggestive of retail-style service to patrons.

Armed with a search warrant, the deputies seized 3,000 bottles of beer and 150 gallons of unbottled beer, all of which took them one and a half hours to destroy after preserving evidentiary samples. Charged with possession of liquor, Radell received a $1,000 fine, but was undeterred by the experience. In May of 1928, Radell's home was raided – for the third time. A jury trial followed, a verdict could not be agreed upon, and without any explanation, no re-trial was ever scheduled.

Nearly four months later, a Lorain County Grand Jury convened. The focus of its investigation was the matter of "protection money" and those who collected it. Speculation was that money was being paid by beer joint and speakeasy owners to "middle men" who were acting on behalf of unscrupulous persons inside prohibition enforcement circles.

---

[11] Stop 55 is in the approximate location of the Avon Lake Public Library.

Although 14 witnesses reportedly testified, the press focused on Neil Radell. His confidence apparently bolstered by his previous successful mistrial, Radell was described as surviving 45 minutes of questioning, after which he "left the courtroom smiling broadly". While Radell may have considered himself the victor, so may have Avon Lake, as the press' report identified Radell as being "formerly of Avon Lake".

Undaunted by the Radell debacle, local law enforcement maintained vigilance in Avon Lake, even as Prohibition continued to stir a cat-and-mouse game with rum-runners. Marshall Carl Tomanek and Deputy Marshall Paul McCampbell both made names for themselves as they thwarted at least some of the booze distribution in their village. In June of 1928, McCampbell spotted suspicious Lake Erie activity offshore at the end of Avon Lake's Fay Avenue.

After patiently observing the repeated approach of a smaller boat to a distant, much larger vessel followed by as many return trips to shore, McCampbell summoned Tomanek. Together, the two scored confiscation of 26 cases of hard liquor and one case of wine, all of which were given over to federal agents.

In August of 1929, Marshall Tomanek's solo efforts resulted in the seizure of 19 cases of Canadian whiskey that had been unloaded behind Avon Lake's illuminating plant. The bust was hailed as the county's largest haul of the year. Tomanek's victory was sweetened by the arrest of two rum-runners associated with transportation of the wares.

Marshall Carl Tomanek.
Photo courtesy of Carl "Timer" Tomanek

Local jubilation over rum running deterrence in the late 1920's was short-lived as the stock market crashed October 29, 1929, and the mood grew somber. Increasingly, Americans were facing job loss, families were forced to share housing, and those without farms struggled to keep food on their tables. Competition for survival extended to the rum-running industry, with an increase in feuds amongst runners. Animosity intensified between runners and Coast Guardsmen who characterized rum-runners as "increasingly defiant".

Coast Guard enforcement was bolstered in February 1930 with the addition of 15 new speedy vessels and a force of 100 men. Their target was the stretch of lake from Lorain to Avon Point. Aside from confiscation of alcohol, capture of the swiftest of the rum-running crafts meant reinforcement of the Coast Guard's own patrol vessels. In their haste to declare victory, Coast Guardsmen drew criticism from yacht owners who complained of being fired upon by Coast Guard crews, who were not always accurate in the profiling of their targets. Guardsmen did little to enhance their reputation when they boasted to the press that they planned to engage in "a little rifle practice" off Avon Lake's shore as a deterrent to alcohol smugglers.

Warring rum-runners were sometimes brutally eliminated in the course of internal feuds. In May of 1930, the body of a man was found washed ashore at Avon Lake's beach. The corpse of his companion – a known rum-runner from Cleveland – was found ashore a short distance west. Both had been severely beaten and left with fractured skulls.

The victims were eventually identified. One was 23-year-old Miles Mandrich, and the other was 21-year-old John Snowbrick, a truck driver with a wife and two baby sons. Whether the inciting vendetta had been fully resolved is unclear, as 11 days later, Snowbrick's mother disappeared from her Cleveland home.

As the battle on rum-running intensified along the lake's shore, street enforcement sought to keep pace. In October 1930, Avon Lake's Lake Road was the site of that year's record haul. Special deputy Leo Heider single-handedly appropriated a truck loaded with 11 kegs of beer on Lake Road. Deputy Heider forced the truck into a ditch and then commandeered the vehicle after its driver and accomplice fled into a dense fog. Heider then delivered the truck and its cargo to Elyria to the custody of Lorain County Sheriff Clarence E. Adams.

Even as Avon Lake's law enforcement agents continued their pursuit of prohibition violators, public opinion of the nation's dry law had soured. Some began to condemn the legislation as a breeding ground for hypocrisy, bribery, corruption, and crime. A reporter for the neighboring *Sandusky Register* lamented that bootlegged alcohol with its various adulterations, which allegedly included denatured alcohol designed for use in an anti-freeze mixture for automobiles, resulted in more deaths than did the consumption of whiskey of pre-prohibition days.

Public opinion prevailed in its anti-dry campaign. The nation bid a festive farewell to the 18th Amendment with passage of its repeal in December 1933. While Avon Lake's marshalls abandoned bootleg chases, one Avon Laker found an open door to a new career – with benefits. Matt Hinkel was about to become Ohio's first government-funded whiskey taster.

Chapter 12

A Taste for Change

Prohibition's displacement of brewers and liquor retailers opened new entrepreneurial opportunities for rum-running and bootlegging. The tables were turned, however, with its repeal. One retailer to emerge unscathed by the 18th Amendment was millionaire boxing promoter and referee Matt Hinkel, who in his final years called Avon Lake his home.

Matt Hinkel, son of a saloon keeper, carried on the family tradition under the name of Hinkel Company, a wholesale and retail dealer of liquor. His was one of the largest wholesale liquor businesses of Cleveland. Buoyed by the financial success of that business, Hinkel transferred his sales skills to automobiles, and operated Matt Hinkel Motor Sales Co. at 6500 Euclid Avenue in Cleveland.

Not satisfied with limiting himself to retail endeavors, Hinkel developed his long-time passion for boxing into yet another successful venture. He distinguished himself as one of Cleveland's most successful fight promoters, and earned national renown as both a boxing promoter and referee. By 1902, he was recognized as having refereed all of the principal matches held in Ohio.

He so firmly aligned himself with the pugilists, that he was known to introduce himself with the phrase, "shake the hand that shook the hand of John L. Sullivan"[12]. His referee services in boxing rings drew great demand in the 1920's in Ohio. His schedule could be challenging, once requiring him to officiate matches at Cleveland Yacht Club, Barberton Elks Club, and Norwalk fair grounds all within the same week.

---

[12] Nicknamed *The Boston Strongboy*, heavyweight John L. Sullivan is remembered as being the last bare-knuckle boxing champion.

"Teach your son boxing", Hinkel encouraged fathers of young men. "He doesn't need to be a professional, but what he will get from boxing is confidence. Whatever success I may have made in life I credit largely to the confidence I got in boxing". Hinkel credited the sport with keeping him on the "straight and narrow" throughout his youth.

Widowed in 1927, Hinkel remarried in 1929 and moved to a residence in Avon Lake. He became disillusioned with the deterioration of professionalism in boxing and its manipulation by the unscrupulous for financial gain. Hinkel had developed a nationwide reputation as an advocate of "clean sports", and he found boxing's decline to be intolerable.

He left his 40-year career in promoting and refereeing, but a Cleveland newspaper characterized Hinkel's "retirement" as far from sedentary. Instead, Hinkel engaged in farm activity that "would prostrate a heavy-weight wrestler" as he worked his grape vineyard and sawed tree trunks into cords of wood at his Avon Lake farm.

Hinkel remained ever a businessman at heart, and as the 18th Amendment marched toward repeal, rumors circulated that he was returning to the wholesale whiskey business. One local paper boldly proclaimed that Hinkel was resuming business with a million dollars' worth of Scotch whiskey as a starter. Hinkel forecast a significant improvement in the quality of "legal" whiskey, which would soon become available to the public. He openly berated the unpalatable wares being offered by drugstores, whose buyers, Hinkel insisted, were incapable of discerning the better quality goods. Hinkel pulled no punches as he postulated that:

"If the state is going to protect the public against bootleggers, it will have to see that the people get decent stuff at a reasonable price, or the bootleggers, who have learned the whisky game and put out better stuff than some of these blends, will stay right with us".

In a surprise turn of events, the Avon Lake resident abandoned the retail business and instead accepted an appointment by Ohio's then-Governor George White on January 5, 1934 as a technical advisor to the state's new Liquor Control Commission. Hinkel and Ohio's new liquor control director were responsible for making wholesale purchases of alcohol for distribution to Ohio stores. Hinkel's first order for legal alcohol was a purchase of $41,000 worth of Scotch whisky from a New York importer. With approval from Ohio's liquor control director, Hinkel procured 1,150 cases to be delivered to warehouses in 5 Ohio cities. From there, the inventory was to be distributed to licensed state liquor stores.

Hinkel was also responsible for supervising tests to ensure quality of all liquors sold throughout the state. For this, he was publicly chided by the press as being the "official taster" for the department. The Avon Laker didn't deny the necessity for tasting hundreds of samples of stock offered by retailers for sale in Ohio's state stores. He did contend, however, that he never swallowed the goods when tasting.

Nine months into his new job, Hinkel boasted that the bootleggers who continued to compete with state retailers were losing ground because their product was substantially inferior to legal liquor. Twelve months into the job, in yet another surprise turn of events, Hinkel announced his departure from the state department to become manager of sales for Glenmore Distilleries of Louisville, Kentucky – an establishment from which the liquor control department had made purchases in excess of $435,000.

Less than two years later, Hinkel died when stricken by a heart attack at the age of 69. Although still a resident of Avon Lake, Hinkel died in a room at a previous residence – the Hollenden in Cleveland. He was remembered by one sports writer as "an institution in Cleveland sporting circles" and a "square shooter". Hinkel's widow retained the Avon Lake property. Her address at the time of her death was listed as 32647 Lake Road.

Matt Hinkel sketch by Edith Newman

Chapter 13

A Racketeer's Hideaway

As Prohibition approached its end in 1933, those who had succumbed to living ruthlessly through non-taxable means sought other avenues of generating untraceable income. Some found their pot of gold in the numbers business. A game of chance originating in the urban ghettos, "policy men" sold chances to customers for a little as one cent each. "Policy" was the name given by the participants, which was a symbolically vague reference to insurance, or an opportunity to score against the odds of a life in poverty. Originally shunned as a black man's game, the men of rum-running days revised their assessment of the practice, and mounted a campaign to capture the prosperity promised by organizing and developing the racket.

The games were generally of two types: one placing a bet could choose his numbers and buy a chance on matching the last three numbers of total bets placed at a major racetrack, or the last three numbers of closing stock market results as listed in the evening paper. Or, he could try his luck on guessing the correct sequence of numbers as drawn from a bag containing numbered balls. A percentage of winnings was paid to the headquarters or "policy house" controlling the operation, with percentages also being paid to the bookies who took the bets, and to the runners who carried the betting slips and money from bookies to headquarters, and the pay-outs to the lucky winners.

Once the pistol-packing men in dark suits and felt fedoras discovered the potential for profitability in the numbers game, a new style of play was born. Percentages to the house increased, "territories" became firmly defined, and a variety of schemes for avoiding payouts developed.

The first numbers gang to emerge in Cleveland was known as "The Big Four". Of the group, three were black, and one was Caucasian. The latter was Frank Hoge, owner of the White Front Provision Company in Cleveland, a meat market that served as an active front for the profitable numbers operation. Hoge had also expanded into the bonding business, frequently providing bail bond services to defendants charged in gambling cases.

By 1930, he and his three partners were the undisputed kingpins of the numbers racket. Their daily take was reportedly $6,000 to $10,000. When word of their success circulated, the Mob took interest and took action.

Hoge was unharmed but was "warned" by the competition when a bomb exploded under the rear porch of his butcher shop on May 26, 1934. Two of Hoge's partners escaped the Mob's elimination of competition when imprisoned for tax evasion and perjury.[13] The third was shot at his home and promptly announced his retirement from the business, returning later as a minor player for the Mob. Hoge not only survived the purge, but was assimilated into a rackets business that fell under new control and emerged as the "Mayfield Road Gang".[14]

---

[13] One of the two died in prison shortly after his incarceration.

[14] Despite Hoge's escape, his "secretary" faced increased risk in the performance of her duties, and was found clubbed into unconsciousness at her home in May of 1938.

The "Mayfields" drew their own unwanted attention, and became the focus of a 1939 secret investigation led by Eliot Ness, Cleveland Safety Director and former Chicago agent instrumental in the incarceration of gangster Al Capone. Ness' sweeping investigation - hailed as the largest of its kind in Cleveland history - focused on extortion, blackmail, terrorism, and vice cases. One name prominently associated with the probe was Frank Hoge.

Following presentation to a Grand Jury of evidence gleaned through Ness' efforts, twenty-three "racketeers and muscle men" were indicted. Although several of the defendants fled and escaped prosecution, multiple trials and convictions ensued. Hoge, however, was acquitted, the judge in his case having deemed him a "victim" of other policy operators.

Even before Ness' campaign, Hoge had been indicted and arrested, and faced trial multiple times, but had on each occasion emerged unscathed. The heat of Ness' tenacity may have proven too much for Hoge, however, as he left his hometown of Cleveland and by 1941, he moved with his family to the shore's edge in Avon Lake – out of Cuyahoga County, and a short boat or car trip back to his center of operations.

While the specifics underlying Hoge's relocation to Avon Lake remain undisclosed, jurisdictional issues may have been an inducement. In January of 1935, Michael McGinty, a lookout for a Cleveland bookie joint, was found dead in his car on Lake Road in Avon Lake. Known by the nicknames "Stiff Hat Eddie" and "Derby" McGinty, he had been stabbed in the face, chest, and arms repeatedly with what appeared to be an ice pick, and his skull had been crushed by a blunt object identified as likely being an ax or a hatchet.

Found inside his derby hat, which had been jammed low on his head, were various policy slips marked with his initials. Speculation stirred as comparisons were made between McGinty's grisly end and two earlier brutal deaths of two policy competitors allegedly perpetrated by the Mayfield Gang. Almost as disturbing as McGinty's brutal murder was the dispute between adjoining jurisdictions regarding responsibility for opening an investigation. Cleveland police maintained that McGinty had been murdered in Avon Lake Village, placing the matter in the hands of Lorain County authorities. Lorain County's Sheriff was convinced, however, that the man had been murdered in Cleveland, and that his corpse had been transported to Avon Lake thereafter, leaving the matter a Cuyahoga County concern. One news reporter simply deemed the matter a casualty of the underworld's own brand of justice.

Whether the rift between Lorain County and Cuyahoga County jurisdictions was Hoge's motive for changing his residence, his Avon Lake location appeared to serve him well. He reputedly continued his control of the infamous Café Tia Juana in Cleveland where the numbers game flourished, was safely distant when the home of his second in command was rocked by dynamite, and ducked the legal system even as his brother and co-conspirator, Willie Hoge, was sent to the penitentiary.

Hoge's success in surviving prosecution and circumventing the legal system stirred the ire of the law-abiding element of the Cleveland community, which continued its efforts to shut him down. A scathing report was issued by a Cuyahoga County Grand Jury in April 1948 on police corruption. The jurors wrote that "Not until Frank and Willie Hoge are shorn of their malignant power will the police department be wholly free from corruption."

Frank Hoge was accused of possessing "extraordinary ability to take a police officer who is vulnerable and put him in a position of accepting a bribe." Hoge's White Front Provision butcher store was again made the target of investigation in September 1949. He persisted in his denials of any wrongdoing, insisting that he was "only a butcher", and disavowing any connection to the activities of his convicted brother and former co-conspirators.

The lake shore home afforded safe haven. Hoge finished out his days there without ever seeing the inside of a prison cell despite his Cleveland notoriety. He did garner more press, however, in December 1951 when he paid in excess of $31,000 to the IRS to avoid tax liens against his property that would have forced him out of the bonding business.

Sketch of Frank Hoge by Edith Newman

The press he drew was never laudatory. While in Avon Lake, he did not make society pages, host social events, or take part in community activities. The only other Avon Lake name associated with Hoge was that of Attorney Thomas Brinsmade, who appeared with Hoge in Cleveland Police Court in 1930 when Hoge fought a bond forfeiture hearing after a woman for whom he had served as bondsman fled and left Hogue at risk of losing $500.

Hoge kept a lower profile in his later life until his death on July 31, 1966, when at the age of 70, he was struck down by a heart attack. His obituary remembered him as being "one of the top policy men in the country at the height of his career." He was described as having devoted "his full attention to the bail bonding business" in his final years - work that had drawn him into the center of a scandal in 1930 for holding a monopoly on the bond business for the Central Police Station.

Frank Hoge's illicit undertakings and daring lifestyle had profited him well. His residence address was listed as 32196 Lake Road in Avon Lake, and an inventory filed in Lorain County Probate Court set his estate's value at $474,361. Though in life Hoge may have instilled fear in many, in death he left open the question of post mortem respect - his obituary was published in the *Plain Dealer* directly below that paper's "Laff-A-Day" cartoon.

Chapter 14

Why?

Avon Lake's history is diverse, its path of creation sinuous, and its characters often colorful. Retracing its trail is both difficult and exhilarating. Perhaps most challenging is the question posited by some: "Why do you care about local history?"

That question might best be answered by viewing history in the context of a probate matter. Were one to discover that he or she had just been left a substantial inheritance by a distant, unknown relative, the fortunate heir would be intrigued by a number of thoughts. Human nature being what it is, the first question would most likely be, "What was left to me?"

Once the inventory was disclosed, a curious heir would likely want to know more about the person who left the legacy. Who was this individual? Where did he or she come from, and how were these assets accumulated?

We are all heirs. We have been left the legacy of Avon Lake, and the curious yearn to know all that their inheritance entails. We are citizen-beneficiaries, and bidden or not, this inheritance connects us to each other and to the past.

We have inherited a community. We are the product of Beach Park revelers and summering captains of industry; laboring farmers and land developers with a cash-fueled plan; visionaries and bootleggers; statesmen and racketeers; the insane and the ingenious; those who embraced national law and values, and those who railed against them. It is this past that makes us unique and sets us apart from other communities. Our identity emerges only as our past is more clearly defined.

And that, inquiring reader, is why local history matters.

I am bound to them,

Though I cannot look into their eyes or

Hear their voices.

I honor their history.

I cherish their lives.

I will tell their story.

I will remember them.

–Author Unknown -

Endnotes

Chapter 1 - Growing Pains

pioneer Noah Davis - Walker, Milburn. *The Avon Lake Story*. Avon Lake, OH: Kiwanas Club of Avon Lake, O., 1965. 9. Print. The Lake Shore Electric Railway fostered Beach Park - Patton, Thomas J., Dennis Lamont, and Albert Doane. *Lake Shore Electric Railway*. Charleston, SC: Arcadia, 2009. 11. Print. court proceedings to enjoin any bifurcation – "They Threaten Injunction", *Plain Dealer* (Cleveland, Ohio), January 22, 1905, 22 July 1911 election was held – "Notice of Election", *The Elyria Telegram* (Elyria, Ohio), June 21, 1911, 3 election on November 7, 1911 – "Avon Lake Will Be A Village Shortly", *The Elyria Telegram* (Elyria, Ohio), December 8, 1911, 4 construction of a brick highway - "Up in the Air", *The Elyria Telegram* (Elyria, Ohio), December 22, 1913, 1 surrender its charter - "Village Would Change Form, Dodge Paving", *The Cleveland Leader* (Cleveland, Ohio), December 31, 1913, 12 the charter was surrendered - "Items", *The Elyria Telegram* (Elyria, Ohio), August 13, 1914, 5 voted for independent incorporation - "Two Villages At Avon Now Foreseen", *The Elyria Telegram* (Elyria, Ohio), April 5, 1917, 6 entitlement to the railroad easement - "Avon And Avon Lake Villages To Fight For Railroad Taxes", *The Elyria Telegram* (Elyria, Ohio), April 6, 1917, 1 Avon Lake prevailed - "Avon Lake Village is Winner in Suit", *The Elyria Telegram* (Elyria, Ohio), June 30, 1917, 1

Chapter 2 - The Encroaching Elite

monotonous drudgery of business – "Grape Growers' Excursion", *The Cleveland Leader* (Cleveland, Ohio), September 8, 1866, 4

1874 map of Avon Lake at Avon Point – *Atlas and Directory of Lorain County, Ohio, Illustrated*, The American Atlas Company, 1896, Cleveland, Ohio

christened the spot "To Kalon Beach" - "Personal", *The Cleveland Leader* (Cleveland, Ohio), August 25, 1888, 6

all migrated to To Kalon each summer through 1890 - "East End", *Plain Dealer* (Cleveland, Ohio), September 7, 1890, 4

Sayle served as director of Midland Bank – Ad, *Plain Dealer* (Cleveland, Ohio), April 5, 1926, 6

manager of the Cleveland Punch and Shear Works – Obituary, *Plain Dealer* (Cleveland, Ohio), September 6, 1941, 17

the family of John Goetz made society news – "Pleasant Affairs", *Plain Dealer* (Cleveland, Ohio), August 7, 1898, 18, 19

latest in hats, bonnets, and millinery - "Charming!", *The Cleveland Leader* (Cleveland, Ohio), October 5, 1890, 9

employees of the latter's store were invited there – "Employees Entertained", *Plain Dealer* (Cleveland, Ohio), July 20, 1898, 3

entertained there in 1901 - "Society", *Plain Dealer* (Cleveland, Ohio), July 28, 1901, 14

his demise on October 10, 1919 – Death Certificate of John Goetz, Ohio Bureau of Vital Statistics, No. 58935

Mrs. Robert Goetz entertained the Garden Club – "News of the Garden Clubs", *Plain Dealer* (Cleveland, Ohio), August 4, 1935, 19

Lilac Ledges, Reidlands – "D.A.R. Guilds Plan Avon Lake Outing", *Plain Dealer* (Cleveland, Ohio), August 3, 1919, 6

general manager of the Strong-Carlisle-Hammond Company – "David E. Parsons Dies", *Plain Dealer* (Cleveland, Ohio), July 13, 1934, 2

her Avon Lake residence more than 100 years old,– "Today's Club Calendar", *Plain Dealer* (Cleveland, Ohio), July 30, 1919, 15

tapestries, heirlooms, antiques and laces valued at over $12,000.00 – "Fire Razes Landmark", *Plain Dealer* (Cleveland, Ohio), May 29, 1927, 31

Mrs. Parsons until her death in 1930– "Death Notice", *Plain Dealer* (Cleveland, Ohio), November 29, 1930, 20

Mr. Parsons until his death in 1934– "David E. Parsons Dies", *Plain Dealer* (Cleveland, Ohio), July 13, 1934, 2

occupied Cliffhurst at least as early as 1909 – "Social News Of The Week", *Plain Dealer* (Cleveland, Ohio), May 30, 1909, 37

Civil War veteran with Co. H of the 150th OVI - "Death Ends Work of Col. Brinsmade", *Plain Dealer* (Cleveland, Ohio), November 17, 1913, 4; "Allan T. Brinsmade Dies At Son's Home", *The Cleveland Leader* (Cleveland, Oh), November 17, 1913, 2

Anna Brinsmade died at Cliffhurst – "Death Notice", *Plain Dealer* (Cleveland, Ohio), August 31, 1910, 11

unflattering press in 1901 – "Father-In-Law Struck Him", *The Cleveland Leader*, July 21, 1901, 15; "Tom Brinsmade Was Arrested", *Plain Dealer* (Cleveland, Ohio), July 21, 1901, 3

charges against Brinsmade were dropped - "Not Enough Evidence", *Plain Dealer* (Cleveland, Ohio), August 1, 1901, 2

position of Cleveland police prosecutor - "Pleasant To Be Free", *Plain Dealer* (Cleveland, Ohio), May 3, 1901, 5

attitude on the liquor question- "Sharpening The Knives", *Plain Dealer* (Cleveland, Ohio), October 1, 1901, 5; "Church Clubs Issue Bulletin", *Plain Dealer* (Cleveland, Ohio), November 2, 1901, 2

bid for office failed - "Democrats Carry The Day In City Of Cleveland And Cuyahoga County", *The Cleveland Leader*, November 6, 1901, 1

a troupe of minstrels in 1907 - "Luna Park Will Be Open Today", *Plain Dealer* (Cleveland, Ohio), May 16, 1907, 2

invest capital in a great proposition . . . in the amusement line – Ad, *Plain Dealer* (Cleveland, Ohio), May 15, 1909, 11

Lillian was granted a divorce – "Divorces Cleveland Attorney", *Plain Dealer* (Cleveland, Ohio), September 17, 1910, 4

In April 1912, Thomas re-married – "Brinsmade Takes Bride", *Plain Dealer* (Cleveland, Ohio), April 18, 1912, 12

defender of more persons in city and county criminal courts than any other lawyer - "T.C. Brinsmade Dies Here At 70", *Plain Dealer* (Cleveland, Ohio), February 15, 1941, 9

his death in 1950 – Obituary, *Plain Dealer* (Cleveland, Ohio), Feruary 14, 1950, 15

primary residence in Cleveland - "Diversions Past And Future", *Plain Dealer* (Cleveland, Ohio), December 4, 1921, 6

fittingly named "Bellmar" - "Gossip of Society", *Plain Dealer* (Cleveland, Ohio), May 9, 1924, 15

site for the couple's dinners and dances - "Pleasant Affairs of Formal or Informal Character", *Plain Dealer* (Cleveland, Ohio), October 19, 1924, 51

Chapter 3 – Avon Point - The Final Destination

recorded Avon Point disasters – "The Discovery and Identification of the Bark *Cortland*", David M. VanZandt, Department of Archaeology, Flinders University, Cleveland Underwater Explorers, ACUA underwater Archaeology Proceedings, 2009

collision of the steamship Morning Star – "Terrible Calamity", *Daily Albany Argus* (Albany, New York), June 24, 1962, 2; "Loss Of The Morning Star", *The Fremont Weekly Journal* (Fremont, Ohio), June 26, 1868, 2; "Casualties, Terrible Lake Disaster", *Cleveland Leader* (Cleveland, Ohio), June 22, 1868, 4

Caroline was one of Isabelle's bridesmaids – "The Lake Erie Disaster - Fate of the Misses Patchen", *Jamestown Journal* (Jamestown, New York), July 3, 1868, 8

in a ceremony held at Trinity Church – "Wedding At Trinity", *Plain Dealer* (Cleveland, Ohio), June 17, 1868, 3

in search of his sisters or their remains – "The Loss Of The Morning Star", *New York Herald*, (New York, New York), June 27, 1868, 5

a trunk identified as belonging to one of the sisters – "The Morning Star, Return of the Wrecking Party-No Bodies Recovered as Yet", *Plain Dealer* (Cleveland, Ohio), June 24, 1868, 3

The friends of those who were lost - *Ashtabula Weekly Telegraph* (Ashtabula, Ohio), June 27, 1868, 2

Caroline's remains were found - "Body Of Miss Patchin Supposed To Be Found", *Cleveland Leader*, (Cleveland, Ohio), September 18, 1868, 4

Mary's body had been found – "From Painesville", *Plain Dealer* (Cleveland, Ohio), October 22, 1868, 2

Lake Erie's waves chant a requiem – "Troy And Its Vicinity", *Daily Albany Argus* (Albany, New York), June 24, 1868, 4

losses included Albert Iddings – "Recovery of Mr. Iddings' Remains", *Plain Dealer* (Cleveland, Ohio), July 6, 1868, 3

near the Avon Point wreck - "Recovery of More Bodies from the Morning Star", *Cincinnati Daily Enquirer* (Cincinnati, Ohio), July 11, 1868, 4

silk top hat – "The Morning Star Disaster. The Latest Particulars--Articles Rescued from the Wrecks", *Plain Dealer* (Cleveland, Ohio), June 23, 1868, 3

never any blame attached to anybody - *The Findlay Jeffersonian* (Findlay, Ohio), June 26, 1868, 2

The Cleveland Leader (Cleveland, Ohio), July 10, 1900,

Tragic loss of human life again struck in 1900, devastating the Corrigan family - Bellamy II, John Stark. Chapter 3, "A Little Excitement." *The Last Days of Cleveland and More True Tales of Crime and Disaster from Cleveland's Past.* Cleveland: Gray, 2010. 69-97. Print; Dutka, Alan F. "Corrigan Family Catastrophes." *Misfortune on Cleveland's Millionaires' Row.* Charleston, SC: History, 2015. 65-74. Print.

Idler also met its demise at Avon Point - "In Cabin Of Idler", *The Cleveland Leader* (Cleveland, Ohio), July 10, 1900, 10

joint family excursion – "Yacht Idler Capsized And Six Perished", *Plain Dealer* (Cleveland, Ohio), July 8, 1900, 1

pleaded with the child's mother – "Taken From The Wreck – The Mother Love", *The Cleveland Leader* (Cleveland, Ohio), July 11, 1900, 5

Mrs. John Corrigan was the only family member to survive - "One Idler Victim At Rest. Services Over the Remains of Miss Etta Irene Corrigan", *Plain Dealer* (Cleveland, Ohio), July 12, 1900, 3

Corrigan brothers hastened to Avon Point - "A Gale Prevents Search For Dead", *Plain Dealer* (Cleveland, Ohio), July 9, 1900, 1

A diver sealed the door and hatchway - "Gale Stops Work On Yacht Idler", *Plain Dealer* (Cleveland, Ohio), July 12, 1900, 3

body of Mrs. James Corrigan was retrieved - "Three Bodies Recovered. Victims of the Idler Taken From the Yacht's Cabin", *Plain Dealer* (Cleveland, Ohio), July 11, 1900, 1

undertaker wagons, which had been summoned by carrier pigeons - "Taken From The Wreck", *The Cleveland Leader* (Cleveland, Ohio), July 11, 1900, 5

Etta's funeral - "One Idler Victim At Rest. Services Over the Remains of Miss Etta Irene Corrigan", *Plain Dealer* (Cleveland, Ohio), July 12, 1900, 3

wreckage was towed 16 miles to Cleveland - "Towing The Yacht Idler In", *Plain Dealer* (Cleveland, Ohio), July 14, 1900, 3; "Idler Is Inside The Breakwater", *Plain Dealer* (Cleveland, Ohio), July 15, 1900, 1

the body of baby Mary was found - "Body Found In Idler's Cabin", *Plain Dealer* (Cleveland, Ohio), July 16, 1900, 1

dispute between Cuyahoga County Coroner and Lorain County Coroner - "The Idler Horror", *The Cleveland Leader* (Cleveland, Ohio), July 9, 1900, 5

body of fifteen-year-old Ida Corrigan - "Another Idler Victim Found. Body of Ida May Corrigan Recovered From the Lake. Picked Up", *Plain Dealer* (Cleveland, Ohio), August 30, 1900, 1   Jane Corrigan's body – "Last Of The Idler Dead", *The Cleveland Leader* (Cleveland, Ohio), September 29, 1900, 10 offering a "liberal reward" for the recovery of bodies – "Reward For Corrigan Bodies Has Been Offered by the Father of the Girls", *Plain Dealer* (Cleveland, Ohio), July 24, 1900, 6; Classified Ads - *Plain Dealer* (Cleveland, Ohio), July 24, 1900, 10; *Plain Dealer* (Cleveland, Ohio), August 11, 1900, 7; *The Cleveland Leader* (Cleveland, Ohio), September 6, 1900, 7

until the remaining family members were found and all could be buried together - "No Recoveries Yesterday", *Plain Dealer* (Cleveland, Ohio), July 17, 1900, 10

buried together in Lakeview Cemetery - "Corrigan Family Buried", *Plain Dealer* (Cleveland, Ohio), October 10, 1900, 3; "A Scene Never To Be Forgotten", *The Cleveland Leader* (Cleveland, Ohio), October 10, 1900, 8

Chapter 4 - A Scrap of the Better Life

Fresh Air Camp was formed by "Father" Addison – "Many Mourners", *Plain Dealer* (Cleveland, Ohio), January 17, 1898, 3

"outing department" was established – "City Waifs Are Coming", *The Elyria Daily Chronicle*, July 2, 1906, 1

returned home after a two weeks' stay – "Tanned And Happy", *Plain Dealer* (Cleveland, Ohio), August 7, 1898, 15

"tagging" of pre-qualified children - "More Homes Wanted for City Waifs", *The Elyria Daily Chronicle* (Elyria, Ohio), July 4, 1906, 9

qualifying student – "Federation of Women's Clubs Plans Picnic For Education Branch Wards", *Plain Dealer* (Cleveland, Ohio), August 1, 1926, 8

annual picnic for the student protégés - "Federation To Entertain Its Protégés", *Plain Dealer* (Cleveland, Ohio), August 11, 1925, 14

graduate of the school of education - Obituary for Mrs. Edward J. Weigel, *Plain Dealer* (Cleveland, Ohio), February 8, 1955, 14

Chapter 5 - Coveting Thy Neighbor's Goods

confiscated the goods- "Special Grand Jury Meets To Pass Upon Theft Of Diamonds", *The Elyria Republican* (Elyria, Ohio), December 2, 1909, 1

conflicting theories were developed – "Were Gems Really Thrown Into Lake", *The Elyria Republican* (Elyria, Ohio), Dec. 16, 1909, 7

face-to-face with a Deputy Sheriff – "Must Serve A Term For The Smith Theft", *The Evening Telegram* (Elyria, Ohio), November 26, 1910, 1

petition of Mary's release – "Convict May Gain Liberty Ere Long", *The Evening Telegram* (Elyria, Ohio), December 2, 1910, 8

Chapter 6 - Green Gables

German brewers in Cleveland who developed family-owned businesses – Obituary of C.E. Gehring, *Plain Dealer* (Cleveland, Ohio), March 6, 1893, 8

John's first wife was Alvie Zangerle – "A West Side Marriage", *Plain Dealer* (Cleveland, Ohio), April 13, 1887, 9

was brought to an abrupt end by her death – "Death of Mrs. Gehring", *Plain Dealer* (Cleveland, Ohio), January 27, 1890, 8

architect Frederick Baird - Cleveland Landmarks Commission - 601 Lakeside Ave. Room 519 - Cleveland, OH 44114, planning.city.cleveland.oh.us/landmark/ .../archdetailPrint.php

the home had finally been named – "About the Town", *Plain Dealer* (Cleveland, Ohio), June 17, 1899, 5; "In Society", *Plain Dealer* (Cleveland, Ohio), June 18, 1899, 30

Gehring loves his country home so well – "About the Town", *Plain Dealer* (Cleveland, Ohio), January 10, 1900, 4

Crafted bits of souvenir artistry - "Clambake at Green Gables", *Plain Dealer* (Cleveland, Ohio), September 15, 1904, 12

ownership of the Hollenden's resident mutt - "Gehring Entertains", *Plain Dealer* (Cleveland, Ohio), September 16, 1906, 6

Bum "wrote" - " 'Bum' Takes Pen In Paw And Writes To Pete", *Plain Dealer* (Cleveland, Ohio), November 2, 1906, 14

Gehring died at his much-loved Green Gables - "Retired Brewer Called by Death", *Plain Dealer* (Cleveland, Ohio), November 4, 1913, 7

Welsh opera star Adelina Patti - "The Queen of Song is Tired of Craig-y-Nos", *Plain Dealer* (Cleveland, Ohio), April 28, 1901, 32

a vocalist and a conductor - "Going in for Music", *Plain Dealer* (Cleveland, Ohio), August 26, 1899, 10; "Concerts", *Plain Dealer* (Cleveland, Ohio), May 26, 1901, 21

financed a trip by the Orpheus Male Choir - "Plan Trip For Orpheans", *Plain Dealer* (Cleveland, Ohio), July 13, 1925, 4

Margaret, who was herself a composer - "Orpheus Chorus Sings Her Song", *Plain Dealer* (Cleveland, Ohio), April 26, 1941, 12

Britain's former Prime Minister, David Lloyd George - "City Will Be Paid New Honor Today By Lloyd George", *Plain Dealer* (Cleveland, Ohio), October 23, 1923, 1, 18

entertainment for the Welsh Club - "Interesting News of the Women's Clubs", *Plain Dealer* (Cleveland, Ohio), August 21, 1921, 7

meetings of the Women's Board of Grace Hospital - "Mrs. E. S. Griffiths Hostess to Grace Hospital Women", *Plain Dealer* (Cleveland, Ohio), July 7, 1929, 43; "Club Activities", *Plain Dealer* (Cleveland, OH), November 3, 1933, 14

Edwin Griffiths died - "E. S. Griffiths Is Dead In Florida", *Plain Dealer* (Cleveland, Ohio), January 26, 1930, 13

hosted a niece's wedding in the Craig-Y-Nos rose garden - "Funk-Burt", *Plain Dealer* (Cleveland, Ohio), July 2, 1933, 30

spring of 1934, the home was listed for sale - "Sale Suburban Property", *Plain Dealer* (Cleveland, Ohio), April 22, 1934, 42

transferred ownership of Craig-Y-Nos to Robert Hildebrandt – "Real Estate Transfers", *Chronicle Telegram* (Elyria, Ohio), May 23, 1934, 8

Charles and Katherine moved into the home - "Avon", *The Chronicle-Telegram* (Elyria, Ohio), June 9, 1934, 8 founded the Hildebrandt Provision Company – Obituary for Charles Hildebrandt, *Chronicle Telegram* (Elyria, Ohio), February 2, 1957, 26

Katherine became involved in her husband's business - "$250,000 in Gifts Draws Tax Study", *Plain Dealer* (Cleveland, Ohio), December 17, 1947, 3

rose to the position of Vice President - Obituary of Charles Hildebrandt, *Plain Dealer* (Cleveland, Ohio), February 2, 1957, 9

Robert Hildebrandt transferred property – "Real Estate Transfers", *The Chronicle-Telegram* (Elyria, Ohio), July 15, 1935, 3

featured a lecture on Williamsburg flowers - "Avon Lake", *The Chronicle-Telegram* (Elyria, Ohio), July 8, 1938, 5

performance by a harpist - "Avon Lake Garden Club Members Hear Clevelander", *The Chronicle-Telegram* (Elyria, Ohio), July 14, 1939, 9

Mathilda died – no caption, *The Chronicle-Telegram* (Elyria, Ohio), November 13, 1944, 2

Catherine married Dr. Orie Mazanec – "Catherine Frances Pfahl Married to Dr. Orie Mazanec", *Plain Dealer* (Cleveland, Ohio), October 17, 1948, 88

Rosemary married Joseph F. Duber - "Rosemary Duber and Joseph F. Pfahl Are Wed Here", *Plain Dealer* (Cleveland, Ohio), June 29, 1952, 88

Katherine died at Green Gables – "Draws Tax Study", *Plain Dealer* (Cleveland, Ohio), December 17, 1947, 3

notice that appeared in the Plain Dealer for Katharina Hildebrandt - *Plain Dealer* (Cleveland, Ohio), February 3, 1947, 7

notice that appeared in the Plain Dealer for Charles Hildebrandt - *Plain Dealer* (Cleveland, Ohio), February 2, 1957, 5

Robert died on March 2, 1965 – Obituary, *Chronicle Telegram* (Elyria, Ohio), March 2, 1965, 14; Obituary, *Plain Dealer* (Cleveland, Ohio), March 3, 1965, 36

Chapter 7 - The Folger House

Thomas Folger was born February 14, 1842 – *History of North Central Ohio: Embracing Richland, Ashland, Wayne, Medina, Lorain, Huron and Knox Counties,* William Alexander Duff, Historical Publishing Company, 1931 - Ohio, Volume 3, 1393
served as Secretary of the United States Treasury – "Folger's Vacation", *Plain Dealer* (Cleveland, OH), August 30, 1883, 1
enlisted in Company H – *History of North Central Ohio: Embracing Richland, Ashland, Wayne, Medina, Lorain, Huron and Knox Counties, supra*
daughters were born to Thomas and Della – United States, Bureau of the Census (24 June 1880). 1880 Census: Thomas Folger Family. Sheet 41-A. Thomas Folger.   Avon, Lorain County, Ohio; enumeration district 162, household 356. Ancestry.com   (http://www.ancestry.com: accessed   26 February 2016).
purchased 155 acres at the lake shore – Selected U.S. Federal Census Non-Population Schedules, 1850-1880, Schedule 2-Productions of Agriculture in Avon, Lorain County, Ohio (24 June 1880). Henry Folger. Page 26, enumeration district 162. Ancestry.com   (http://www.ancestry.com: accessed   26 February 2016)
Della and Eliza purchased 63 acres - "Real Estate Transfers", *The Elyria Democrat* (Elyria, Ohio), September 16, 1875, 3
"strange old house" – "Former Elyria Mayor, Veteran of Civil War, Builder of Town Hall", *Chronicle Telegram* (Elyria, Ohio), April 4, 1955, 16
Henry died at Thomas' Elyria residence – Obituary, *The Elyria Republican* (Elyria, Ohio), November 29, 1883, 2
served Elyria as a councilman - "The Republican Factions are After Each Other's Scalps", *Plain Dealer* (Cleveland, Ohio), June 27, 1891, 4; "Democratic Caucus at Elyria", *Plain Dealer* (Cleveland, Ohio), March 14, 1894, 3
manager of the Lorain County Grape Growers' Shipping Association – "Lorain County Grape Industry", *The Elyria Republican* (Elyria, Ohio), January 4, 1894, 4

gave his eldest daughter, Anna, in marriage – "Braman-Folger", *Plain Dealer* (Cleveland, Ohio), June 21, 1895, 7

president of the Savings Deposit Bank and Trust Company - Elyria, Ohio, City Directory, 1923, U.S. City Directories, Ancestry.com, Online publication - Provo, UT, USA: Ancestry.com Operations, Inc.

nuptials of daughter Josephine – "Will Be Married in Elyria", *The Cleveland Leader* (Cleveland, Ohio), November 22, 1895, 2; "Two Well-Known Young People of Elyria United in Marriage", *The Cleveland Leader* (Cleveland, Ohio), December 5, 1895, 3

involved in the Elyria banking business - "Happened In Lorain", *The Cleveland Leader* (Cleveland, Ohio), February 11, 1896, 4

40 acres of grapes at his Avon Point farm – "Northern Ohio Grapes", *Plain Dealer* (Cleveland, Ohio), July 31, 1898, 9

Folger being the representative of one of those – "Grape Growers", *The Cleveland Leader* (Cleveland, Ohio), July 12, 1899, 7

escorted his last daughter down the aisle – "Bride For Cleveland", *The Cleveland Leader* (Cleveland, Ohio), June 15, 1900, 2; "Wedded An Elyria Girl", *Plain Dealer* (Cleveland, Ohio), June 15, 1900, 15

new thirty-room residence – "Summer Residence", *The Elyria Reporter* (Elyria, Ohio), September 19, 1901, 2

enjoying their new summer residence – "Personal Mention", *The Elyria Republican* (Elyria, Ohio), June 26, 1902, 8

solo return trip to his Elyria home - "He Was Not A Burglar", *The Elyria Republican* (Elyria, Ohio), August 21, 1902, 1

resulted in his nomination for mayor of Elyria - "Elyria Democratic Ticket", *Plain Dealer* (Cleveland, Ohio), March 17, 1903, 5

billed by the *Elyria Reporter* newspaper as "a stinging rebuke"– "A Stinging Rebuke", *The Elyria Reporter* (Elyria, Ohio), April 7, 1903, 1

softened the announcement of victory – "The Election", *The Elyria Republican* (Elyria, Ohio), April 9, 1903, 4 first case in mayor's court - "The First Arrest Under Mayor Folger", *The Elyria Reporter* (Elyria, Ohio), May 4, 1903, 1

tramps brought to mayor's court - "Tramps Will Work", *The Chronicle* (Elyria, Ohio), May 9, 1903, 1, 6; "Police Court", *The Chronicle* (Elyria, Ohio), July 9, 1904, 1

was going to sue Folger for false imprisonment - "Hobo vs. The City", *The Chronicle* (Elyria, OH), May 9, 1903, 3

an undesirable port for tramps to steer - (no caption) *The Weekly Chronicle* (Elyria, Ohio), May 15, 1903, 4

an old soldier appeared before Folger - "Fanatic Arrested", *The Chronicle* (Elyria, Ohio), May 28, 1903, 6

Folger's patience wore thin - "Thirty Minutes", *The Chronicle* (Elyria, Ohio), August 29, 1903, 1

no tolerance in cases of animal abuse - "For Cruelty to a Horse", *The Elyria Republican* (Elyria, Ohio), June 18, 1903, 3; "Abused His Horse", *The Elyria Reporter* (Elyria, Ohio), August 27, 1903, 8; "Fined On Humane Charge", *The Elyria Reporter* (Elyria, Ohio), August 8, 1903, 1

defendant who stole a litter of pups - "Stole Three Hound Pups", *The Chronicle* (Elyria, Ohio), June 10, 1903, 20

stole a woman's pet poodle - "Umbrella Mender Stole A Poodle", *The Elyria Reporter* (Elyria, Ohio), June 18, 1904, 1

men who abandoned or failed to support their wives and children - "Fined For Neglect of Family", *The Chronicle* (Elyria, Ohio), July 22, 1903, 1; "Parole", *The Weekly Chronicle* (Elyria, Ohio), October 9, 1903, p. 6; "Fined For Neglect", *The Chronicle* (Elyria, Ohio), May 9, 1904, 1

a warning regarding proper swim attire - "Bathers Arrested", *The Elyria Reporter* (Elyria, Ohio), July 16, 1903, 5

a song and dance routine - "Paid With Song And Dance", *The Elyria Republican* (Elyria, Ohio), December 3, 1903, 1

nominate him as a candidate for State Senator - "The Mayor Will Not Be A Candidate For State Senator", *The Elyria Reporter* (Elyria, Ohio), September 8, 1903, 1

prison reform congress held in Kentucky - "Compliment Paid by Governor Nash to Mayor Folger", *The Elyria Reporter* (Elyria, Ohio), September 26, 1903, 1

"magic chair" lecture - "Wonderful Is Mayor Folger's Magic Chair", *The Elyria Reporter* (Elyria, Ohio), March 16, 1905, 8

remained actively involved with the grape growers association – "Grape Growers Will Fight, Mayor of Elyria at Head of New Association", *Plain Dealer* (Cleveland, Ohio), August 29, 1905, 10

first announced his intent to seek re-election - "Folger Announces His Candidacy", *The Elyria Reporter* (Elyria, Ohio), June 7, 1905, 4

friction within the Democratic Party - "Democrats Want Active Campaign", *The Elyria Reporter* (Elyria, Ohio), September 9, 1905, 1

announced his retirement - "Mayor Folger Retires", *The Elyria Republican* (Elyria, Ohio), October 28, 1905, 4; "Folger Declines Second", *The Plain Dealer* (Cleveland, Ohio), September 27, 1905, 3

plan to build a distillery - "Distillery Is To be Built At Avon", *The Elyria Reporter* (Elyria, Ohio), October 23, 1906, 6

castoff produce for distillation would be grapes that spoiled - "Use Spoiled Grapes To Make Alcohol, Ex-Mayor Folger Has a Scheme for Utilizing Waste Fruit Products of Avon", *The Elyria Republican* (Elyria, Ohio), November 8, 1907, 1

mayoral candidate for a second term - "Democrats Decide To Support Folger For Mayor's Office", *The Elyria Republican* (Elyria, Ohio), August 5, 1909, 5

Folger died of a heart attack - "Thomas Folger, Mayoralty Candidate, Dies Suddenly At His Summer Home", *The Elyria Republican* (Elyria, Ohio), October 14, 1909, 1

Chapter 8 - Beach Park Ballyhoo

Avon Lake's renowned Beach Park resort - "Initial Trip To Cleveland", *The Cleveland Leader* (Cleveland, Ohio), September 15, 1897, 2

one of the most beautiful of the suburban resorts – Ad, *Plain Dealer* (Cleveland, Ohio) , March 12, 1899, 27 cater to a better class –"Avon Beach Park", *Elyria Republican* (Elyria, Ohio), February 24, 1910, 3; Ad, *Plain Dealer* (Cleveland, Ohio), April 30, 1910, 7

merry-go-round became unfortunate casualty – "Stands And Tents Blown Away", *Plain Dealer* (Cleveland, Ohio) , July 31, 1901, 5

Sunday school picnics – "140 In Baptist Excursion Today", *The Evening Telegram* (Elyria, Ohio), July 17, 1907, 1; "Presbyterian Picnic At Avon Beach Park", *Elyria Evening Telegram* (Elyria, Ohio), July 17, 1917, 2; "Grace Evangelicals Plan Outing", *Elyria Evening Telegram* (Elyria, Ohio), July 17, 1917, 2

boating, fishing, bathing, billiards, baseball, bowling – Ad, *Plain Dealer* (Cleveland), May 22, 1921, 8

funny laughing mirrors – Ad, *Plain Dealer* (Cleveland), July 2, 1921, 16

greased pig – Ad, *Elyria Reporter* (Elyria, Ohio), August 24, 1907, 1

Local 235 - "Lorain County's Master Horse Shoe-ers", *Elyria Reporter* (Elyria, Ohio), August 12, 1904, 1

dancing masters of the West Side – "Recreation And Amusement", *The Cleveland Leader* (Cleveland, Ohio), April 14, 1901, 15

city dwellers hungered for recreational activity – Dulles, Foster Rhea. *A History of Recreation; America Learns to Play*. New York: Appleton-Century-Crofts, 1965. 336-48. Print.

changing to rain and through the mist at Niagara Falls – Ad, *Plain Dealer* (Cleveland, Ohio), April 27, 1919, 13

hosted lively Scottish dances - "1,500 Scots At Outing", *The Cleveland Leader* (Cleveland, Ohio), July 27, 1913, 2

The West Side Master Plumbers – "Plumbers To Picnic", *Plain Dealer* (Cleveland, Ohio), July 30, 1922, 38

employees of the Higbee Co. store - "Fill Nine Specials To Take In Outing", *Plain Dealer* (Cleveland, Ohio), August 3, 1913, 4B

attack on a local man as he departed Beach Park premises – "Avon", The Elyria Reporter (Elyria, Ohio), August 31, 1899, 8

1894 local option vote – "Lorain Gained A Hundred", *The Cleveland Leader* (Cleveland, Ohio), November 8, 1894, 3

hosted meetings of the Women's Christian Temperance Union
- "Avon Lake", *The Elyria Democrat* (Elyria, Ohio), May 27, 1897
arguments advanced by opponents – "Put Off. Action On The
Anti-Screen Ordinance Is Postponed", *The Cleveland Leader*
(Cleveland), June 15, 1897, 2
WCTU's semi-annual convention - "County WCTU Meets", *The
Elyria Republican* (Elyria, Ohio), May 10, 1900, 1
a special election was set - "Avon", *The Chronicle* (Elyria, Ohio),
March 12, 1903, 3
captioned the election story - "Saloon Brawl May 'Dry' Avon",
Plain Dealer (Cleveland, Ohio), March 23, 1903, 9
inconveniences and property value decline - "Avon Township
For Saloons", *Plain Dealer* (Cleveland), March 26, 1903, 1
continue to bear her present unsavory reputation – "Avon
Lake", *Chronicle* (Elyria, Ohio), March 26, 1903
Beach Park may continue to sell liquor - "Avon Township For
Saloons", *Plain Dealer* (Cleveland), March 26, 1903, 1
letter by Rev. Father A. B. Stuber - "Letters From The People",
Plain Dealer (Cleveland, Ohio), March 26, 1903, 5

Chapter 9 - Unhinged at Beach Park

engaged in a bizarre rampage against the townspeople –
"Insane Man Shoots At Avon Beach Residents", *The Elyria
Reporter* (Elyria, Ohio), August 31, 1905, 1
firing at them with a pistol – "Maniac in Lorain", *The Cleveland
Leader*, (Cleveland, Ohio), September 1, 1905, 2
inciting panic amongst the dancers - "Luckily His Aim Is Poor",
Plain Dealer (Cleveland, Ohio), September 1, 1905, 1
escape without shooting him - "Burns House, Shoots Girl", *The
Cleveland Leader*, (Cleveland, Ohio), September 2, 1905, 3
home of the man's parents in Beach Park – "Reign of Terror",
Plain Dealer (Cleveland, Ohio), September 3, 1905, 1
described by the Canton Repository - "Terror In Lorain County
Ended By Maniac's Death", *The Canton Repository* (Canton,
Ohio), September 3, 1905, 13

Emma Pitts, was adjudicated insane – "Adjudged Insane", *The Elyria Reporter* (Elyria, Ohio), April 27, 1905, 5

received the command personally - "Emma Pitts Of Avon Said She Must Kill Someone", *Plain Dealer* (Cleveland, Ohio), October 22, 1905, 5

shoot Dr. Pipes – "Aunt of Peter Pitts Also Becomes Manic", *The Elyria Republican* (Elyria, Ohio), October 26, 1905, 3

died there in May of the following year – "Death of Mrs. Pitts", *The Elyria Reporter* (Elyria, Ohio), May 2, 1906, 1

adjudicated insane in 1906 - "Third Member of Pitts Family Violently Insane", *The Elyria Reporter* (Elyria, Ohio), July 7, 1906, 1

three in succession – "Boy Terror's Uncle Pronounced Insane", *The Elyria Reporter* (Elyria, Ohio), April 13, 1910, 1

victim of a tragic fire – "Seven Victims", *The Cleveland Leader* (Cleveland, Ohio), October 14, 1887, 8

Ads beckoned the curious – Ad, *Plain Dealer* (Cleveland, Ohio), July 3, 1910, 31; Ad, *The Elyria Reporter* (Elyria, Ohio), June 8, 1912, 6

follow the crowd – Ad, *The Evening Telegram* (Elyria, Ohio), June 22, 1912, 5

spectators gathered to watch – "Falls 1,000 Feet; Drowns", *The Democratic Banner* (Mount Vernon, Ohio), May 26, 1914, 1; "Bride Sees Fall to Death", *The Chanute Daily Tribune* (Chanute, Kansas), May 27, 1914, 1; "5,000 See Tragedy", *The Daily Times* (New Philadelphia, Ohio), May 25, 1914, 8

his young bride of five months - "Convinced His Son Is Dead", *The Piqua Daily Call* (Piqua, Ohio), May 26, 1914, 10

22 year old William Warner – "Telegram From Cleveland", *The Piqua Daily Call* (Piqua, Ohio), May 27, 1914, 4

pinned to the lake bottom - "Search Has Been Without Result", *The Piqua Daily Call* (Piqua, Ohio), May 28, 1914, 11

order by the state industrial commission – "Pays For Death Caused By Neglect", *Plain Dealer* (Cleveland, Ohio), August 21, 1914, 6

Chapter 10 - The Demise of Beach Park

plans to construct a new plant - "Avon Beach Site Purchased", *Plain Dealer* (Cleveland, OH), March 5, 1924, 26

a cost of $30,000,000.00 - "Plan $30,000,000 Power Project", *Canton Repository* (Canton, Ohio), November 16, 1924, 10

one of the five biggest - "Lake Cool, They Get Superpower", *Plain Dealer* (Cleveland, Ohio), November 20, 1924, 12

hype to market their property - Ad, *Plain Dealer* (Cleveland, Ohio), November 24, 1924, 20

CEI initiated eminent domain proceedings - "Jury Makes Long Hike", *Plain Dealer* (Cleveland, Ohio), January 21, 1925, 6

Construction proceeded in March of 1925 - "Avon Plant Is Started", *Plain Dealer* (Cleveland, Ohio), March 28, 1925, 18

The CEI hype was capped on August 4, 1926 - "In Step With Progress", *Plain Dealer* (Cleveland, Ohio), August 25, 1926, 6

promise of the development of "Dreamland Beach" - Ad, *Plain Dealer* (Cleveland, Ohio), May 22, 1925, 30

"Dreamland Beach" to be constructed - "Airplane Will Do Stunts And Band Will Play", *Plain Dealer* (Cleveland, Ohio), May 24, 1925, 31

another festively-fused event was promoted by Gayitch - Ad, *Plain Dealer* (Cleveland, Ohio), June 7, 1925, 42

Chapter 11 - 1920's Roar on the Shore

"Districts" were established amongst rum-runners –Okrent, Daniel. *Last Call: The Rise and Fall of Prohibition*. New York: Scribner, 2010. Print; "Systematic Methods Adopted by Rum Runners Operating in This County", *The Chronicle* (Elyria, Ohio), February 1, 1921, 1

Dr. F. M. McMechan, an Avon Lake practitioner - "Doctor Raps U.S. Rules On Use Of Medicinal Liquor", *Plain Dealer* (Cleveland, Ohio), October 17, 1922, 1

operator of a "soft drink parlor" - "Rum Possessor is Fined", *Plain Dealer* (Cleveland, Ohio), March 27, 1923, 24

Lorain-Cleveland "booze route" - "Police Believe They Have Uncovered Lorain-Cleveland Booze Route", *Plain Dealer* (Cleveland, Ohio), March 29, 1924, 18

Avon Lake's Mayor Howard Walker busy - "Fines 5 in Sunrise Court", *Plain Dealer* (Cleveland, Ohio), June 16, 1924, 11

news broke on September 18, 1924 – "Find Bodies, Rum Pirates Are Suspected", *The Daily Times* (New Philadelphia, Ohio), September 18, 1924, 1; "Fear Man and Wife Drowned in Lake Erie", *The Coshocton Tribune* (Coshocton, Ohio), September 18, 1924, 9; "Bodies In Lake Erie Tragedy Are Recovered", *Portsmouth Daily Times* (Portsmouth, Ohio), September 19, 1924, 10

sought shore by tender - "Coast Guard Makes A Thorough Search", *The Evening Repository* (Canton, Ohio), September 19, 1924, 18

Thayers had been the target of rum-runners – "Federal Authorities Probe Death of Clevelanders", *Portsmouth Daily Times* (Portsmouth, Ohio), September 20, 1924, 11

expanded to include an assault on gambling - "2 Aids Fined $100", *Plain Dealer* (Cleveland, Ohio), March 5, 1926, 2

flames breaking into the first floor of the former Black Whale Inn - "Lake Road Homes Burn In Night Fire", *Plain Dealer* (Cleveland, Ohio), March 16, 1926, 1

reportedly in search of a "firebug" - "Seek Firebug", *Portsmouth Daily Times* (Portsmouth, Ohio), March 16, 1926, 1

the inn proclaimed itself one of the area's finest - "Carlton Terrace Management Takes Over Lake Road Inn", *Plain Dealer* (Cleveland, Ohio), May 27, 1923, Women's Section

Lake Road Inn's entertainment featured rising stars – Ad for Guy Lombardo's appearance, *Plain Dealer* (Cleveland, Ohio), May 28, 1924, 18; Ad for Herb Weidoeft's appearance, *Plain Dealer* (Cleveland, Ohio), August 31, 1924, 6

raid was successfully conducted – "Raid Nets $2,500 Gambling Devices", *Plain Dealer* (Cleveland, Ohio), July 7, 1926, 10

burned to the ground – "Lake Road Inn Destroyed", *Repository* (Canton, Ohio), October 14, 1926, 10

Blossom Heath was burned to the ground - "Blaze Destroys New Roadhouse", *Plain Dealer* (Cleveland, Ohio), May 9, 1927, 8

"mansion" of Neil Radell - "Rankin Makes Big Haul At Avon Lake", *The Chronicle*, (Elyria, Ohio), August 15, 1927, 1

received a $1,000.00 fine - "Avon Lake Man Fined $1,000", *The Chronicle*, (Elyria, Ohio), August 30, 1927, 1

Radell's home was raided for the third time – "To Face Grand Jury For 3rd Offense", *The Chronicle*, (Elyria, Ohio), May 25, 1928, 1; "18 True Bills", *The Chronicle*, (Elyria, Ohio), June 14, 1928, 1; "It's Same Old Story", (Plain Dealer, Cleveland, OH), July 11, 1928, 19

the matter of "protection money" - "Hint Lorain Rum Ring Protection", *The Chronicle* (Elyria, Ohio), October 3, 1928, 8

local law enforcement maintained vigilance in Avon Lake - "Marshalls Fire on Man Discovered Unloading Liquor on Beach at Stop 52", *The Chronicle* (Elyria, Ohio), June 8, 1928, 1

Marshall Tomanek's solo efforts - "Confiscate 19 Cases of Liquor", *The Chronicle* (Elyria, Ohio), August 20, 1929, 1

planned to engage in "a little rifle practice" - "No Yo Ho Stuff In Rum Chasing", *Plain Dealer* (Cleveland, Ohio), April 21, 1927, 6

bodies of two men were found at Avon Lake's beach - "Death of Ohio Pair Laid To Rum Feud", *Repository* (Canton, Ohio), May 20, 1930, 13; "2 Deaths Laid To Booze War", *The Sandusky Register* (Sandusky, Ohio), May 20, 1930, 1

mother disappeared from her Cleveland home - "Hunt Missing Mother", *Plain Dealer* (Cleveland, Ohio), May 31, 1930, 19

Special deputy Leo Heider single-handedly appropriated - "Seizes 11 Kegs Of Beer", *Plain Dealer* (Cleveland, Ohio), October 11, 1930, 22

public opinion of the nation's dry law – "Denounce Prohibition", *The Sandusky Register* (Sandusky, Ohio), February 21, 1930, 1

bootlegged alcohol – "50 Sleuths Raid Poison Booze Joints", *The Sandusky Register* (Sandusky, Ohio), June 11, 1930, 1

Chapter 12 – A Taste for Change

millionaire boxing promoter and referee – "Who'll Win?", *The Daily Northwestern* (Oshkosh, Wisconsin), April 22, 1921, 13

one of Cleveland's most successful fight promoters - "Time Passes By", by W.G. Vorpe, *Plain Dealer* (Cleveland, Ohio), October 4, 1936, 95

"shake the hand" – "Death Overtakes Matt Hinkel, 69", *The Canton Repository* (Canton, Ohio), September 21, 1936, 7

refereed all of the principal matches in Ohio - "Wrestling", *The Cleveland Leader* (Cleveland, Ohio), January 19, 1902, 11

and all within the same week – "Matt Hinkel To Be Busy", *Plain Dealer* (Cleveland, Ohio), June 3, 1922, 15

teach your sons –" 'Teach Your Boy How to Box' Matt Hinkel Tells Clubmen", *Plain Dealer* (Cleveland, Ohio), May 27, 1922, 16

moved to a residence in Avon Lake - "Sport Profiles – Hinkel, Retired After 40 Years in Boxing Game, Turns Energy to Cultivating Farm", Al Silverman, *Plain Dealer* (Cleveland, Ohio), December 22, 1932, 15

disillusioned with the deterioration of professionalism in boxing – "Sport Profiles", *ibid.*

engaged in farm activity that "would prostrate a heavy-weight wrestler" – "Sport Profiles", *ibid.*

rumors circulated - "Veterans Of Wine Are Counting Days", Paul L. Einstein, *Plain Dealer* (Cleveland, Ohio), September 20, 1933, 7

pulled no punches as he postulated - "Hinkel Sees State Improving Liquor", *Plain Dealer* (Cleveland, Ohio), December 17, 1933, 2

million dollars' worth of Scotch whiskey – "Veterans Of Wine Are Counting Days", *op. cit.*

technical advisor to Ohio's new Liquor Control Commission - "Matt Hinkel Will Advise Liquor Board", *Plain Dealer* (Cleveland, Ohio), January 5, 1934, 1

a purchase of $41,000 worth of Scotch whisky – "Ohio Orders $41,000 Worth Of 'Scotch'", *Mansfield News* (Mansfield, Ohio), February 3, 1934, 2

"official taster" - "Matt Hinkel To 'Protect' Ohio Liquor Board", *The Sandusky Register* (Sandusky, Ohio), January 5, 1934, 1

never swallowed the goods – "Tastes Liquor Every Day But Doesn't Drink", *Mansfield News* (Mansfield, OH), January 31, 1934, 6

bootleggers who continued to compete - "Hinkel Claims Bootleggers Losing Ground", *Mansfield News* (Mansfield, OH), September 8, 1934, 2

announced his departure from the state department – "Hinkel Is Whiskey Salesman", *The Newark Advocate* (Newark, Ohio), January 21, 1935, 9

died in the Hollenden - "Matt Hinkel Dies Suddenly At 69", *Plain Dealer* (Cleveland, Ohio), September 22, 1936, 28

remembered by one sports writer – "Time Passes By", by W.G. Vorpe, *Plain Dealer* (Cleveland, Ohio), October 4, 1936, 95

Chapter 13 - A Racketeer's Hideaway

A game of chance originating in urban ghettos – Newton, Michael. *Mr. Mob: The Life and Crimes of Moe Dalitz*. Jefferson, NC: McFarland & Company, 2009. Print.

The games were generally of two types – Perry, Douglas. *Eliot Ness: The Rise and Fall of an American Hero*. New York: Viking, 2014. Print.

known as "The Big Four" – *Eliot Ness: The Rise and Fall of an American Hero, supra*

daily take was reportedly $6,000 to $10,000 - *Mr. Mob: The Life and Crimes of Moe Dalitz , supra*; "Checking Over the News of the Week", Russell H. Reeves, *Plain Dealer* (Cleveland, Ohio), October 26, 1931, 12

escaped the Mob's elimination of competition – "Policy Racket Is On Its Last Legs", *Plain Dealer* (Cleveland, Ohio), November 13, 1932, 11

emerged as the Mayfield Road Gang - *Eliot Ness: The Rise and Fall of an American Hero, supra*

found clubbed into unconsciousness - "Woman Clubbed", *The Sandusky Register* (Sandusky, Ohio), May 7, 1938, 12

the focus of a 1939 secret investigation - *Eliot Ness: The Rise and Fall of an American Hero, supra*; "23 in Cuyahoga County Indicted", *The Evening Review* (East Liverpool, Ohio), April 26, 1939, 1; "Police Sweep Games", *The Daily Times* (New Philadelphia, Ohio), April 26, 1939, 1

indicted, arrested, and faced trial - "Smash Hoge Power, Grand Jury Asks", *Plain Dealer* (Cleveland, Ohio), April 28, 1948, 1, 7

Michael McGinty, a lookout for a Cleveland bookie joint - "Body Of Victim Found In Auto", *The Evening Independent* (Massilon, Ohio), January 11, 1935, 1; "Body of Cleveland Man Found Stabbed", *Repository* (Canton, Ohio), January 11, 1935, 18

jurisdictional issues may have been an inducement - "Police Cold On M'Ginty Slaying", *Plain Dealer* (Cleveland, Ohio), January 12, 1935, 1

stabbed in the face, chest, and arms - "Ice Pick Used To Kill Racketeer", *The Charleston Daily Mail* (Charleston, W. Virginia), January 20, 1935, 24

skull had been crushed - "Torn Sleeve Is Clue To Killing", *The Sandusky Register* (Sandusky, Ohio), January 12, 1935, 1

rocked by dynamite - "Dynamite Blasts Rock 2 Homes in Cleveland", *The Circleville Herald* (Circleville, Ohio), September 12, 1949, 2

Willie Hoge was sent to the penitentiary - "Gangland Empire Totters", *Plain Dealer* (Cleveland, Ohio), July 29, 1949, 7

Scathing report issued by a Cuyahoga County Grand Jury - "Smash Hoge Power, Grand Jury Asks", *Plain Dealer* (Cleveland, Ohio), April 28, 1948, 1, 7

butcher store was again made the target of investigation - "Frank Hoge Sees Blackwell Squad", *Plain Dealer* (Cleveland, Ohio), September 1, 1949, 2

Avoid tax liens - "Gambler Pays Tax", *News-Journal* (Mansfield, Ohio), December 8, 1951, 1

Attorney Thomas Brinsmade, who appeared with Hoge – "Hoge Surrenders Fugitive Woman", *Plain Dealer* (Cleveland, Ohio), December 28, 1930, 7
Frank Hoge obituary – *Plain Dealer*, August 2, 1966, 40
set his estate's value at $474,361 – "$474,361 left by Frank Hoge", *Chronicle Telegram* (Elyria, Ohio), December 29, 1966, 2

Made in the USA
Charleston, SC
12 September 2016